The M

Robin Greenwood was born in Scarborough in Yorkshire. At present he is Provincial Officer in the Church of Wales, Chair of the Continuing Ministerial Education and Development Panel of the Ministry Division of the Archbishop's Council, and a Director of the Edward King Institute for Ministry Development. Widely experienced in parish ministry, a member of the Third Order of the Society of St Francis, he has been Diocesan Missioner and Canon Residentiary in Gloucester and has maintained an awareness of developments in academic theology. Author of *Transforming Priesthood* and *Practising Community*, Dr Greenwood has resourced many conferences and workshops in Britain as well as in Australia, Kenya, Sweden, and the USA. He is married to Claire, a psychosexual therapist and trainee psychotherapist. They have three children.

Also by the author
Reclaiming the Church (Fount Original 1986)
Transforming Priesthood (SPCK 1994)
Practising Community (SPCK 1996)

The Ministry Team Handbook

Robin Greenwood

Group exploration for:

- working with God for the well-being of the world

- becoming a ministering community

- developing local, collaborative, mutual, total ministry

- encouraging a deeper partnership between clergy and laity

- growing dynamic leadership in mission for church and world

- sustaining local ministry teams as they evolve

- introducing ordained local ministry as part of a team.

Published in Great Britain in 2000 by
Society for Promoting Christian Knowledge
Holy Trinity Church, Marylebone Road, London NW1 4DU

Second impression 2001

Bible quotations are from *The New Revised Standard
Version of the Bible* © 1989, 1995.

British Library Cataloguing-in-Publication Data

A catalogue record for this book is available from the
British Library

ISBN 0-281-05279-4

Typeset by David Gregson Associates, Beccles, Suffolk

Printed in Great Britain by The Cromwell Press,
Trowbridge, Wiltshire

Contents

To my children – Peter, Tim and Katherine,
and in memory of Hugh G. Woodall,
the priest who set me on the way

Preface

I take pleasure in expressing thanks to the many people whose insight, criticism and support lie behind this handbook. The basic core of this work took shape in dialogue with the Bishop of Chelmsford's Working Group on Local Ministry (1997–99): Shirley Cutbush, Rosemary Enever, Laura Garnham, Cilla Hawkes, Veronica Hydon, Roger Matthews, Peter Nokes, Richard More, David Parrott and Philip Ritchie.

I am grateful for this opportunity to thank members of the Chelmsford Diocesan Resource Team and others whose vision and practical suggestions have influenced the text: Christopher Burdon, Alison Davies, Anne Davison, Alan Edwards, Tom Ely, Eileen French, Mary Grisdale, Joy Halstead, Peter Harding, Peter Hartley, David Jennings, John March, Lynn Money, Julia Mourant, Brian Pepper, David Phillips, Don Phillips, Bridget Ramsay, David Sceats, Julia Shay, John Suddards, Gillian Swift, Martin Wallace and Margaret Withers.

This handbook also has many close connections with the Local Ministry vision of Gloucester Diocese, where I was Diocesan Missioner and Director of Lay Training for nine years. Special appreciation goes to successive Bishops of Gloucester, John Yates, Peter Ball and David Bentley, and to Caroline Pascoe the Local Ministry Officer and Ordained Local Ministry Scheme Principal. This work has been strengthened and quietly encouraged by regular discussions with Professor Daniel W. Hardy. The very character of Local Ministry assumes networking, so that although the final responsibility for the text remains with me, it is the result of a great deal of mutual exchange.

My thanks go also to Jenny Robinson and Ros Giddings for their word processing skills and commitment to this project, and to Robin Keeley and Liz Marsh of SPCK for their clarity and enthusiasm.

Foreword

I am delighted to commend this handbook to clergy, church councils and churches, generally, for careful study and hopefully to stimulate action. It has arisen out of the particular setting of the Anglican Diocese of Chelmsford. This huge and complex Diocese includes the whole of Essex, and five East London boroughs. In the setting of churches large and small, from scattered rural to urban priority, the Diocese of Chelmsford has a strategy for developing the mission and ministry of local churches which takes account of the gifts, responsibilities and opportunities for service of every Christian in the world and the Church.

This handbook, which Canon Robin Greenwood has now edited as a tool for any church or group of churches to use, offers a secure and clear process for groups of clergy and laity to study together. It is rooted in the Five Marks of Mission adopted by the General Synod of the Church of England:

- **To proclaim the good news of the Kingdom.**

- **To teach, baptize and nurture new believers.**

- **To respond to human need by loving service.**

- **To seek to transform the unjust structures of society.**

- **To strive to safeguard the integrity of creation and to sustain and renew the life of the earth.**

To implement these Marks of Mission, the Diocese of Chelmsford has given itself the priorities of the development of churches which are committed to mission through the partnership of laity and clergy in local ministry, through a varied and deepening spirituality rooted in the Triune God, against the background of the Church world-wide. This strategy arises from a way of seeing the mission and ministry of the whole people of God locally as in the Early Church, and reflects the continuing task of the Church in this new Millennium.

In this handbook, Robin Greenwood offers many resources for churches to use as they seek to strengthen or rediscover their vocation as a serving community in response to the commission of Jesus Christ. You will find here a fluid mixture of questions and stimuli to set you thinking and planning for mission, evangelism and ministry in the place in which your church is set. The simple trinitarian dynamic – of diversity in unity – releases the energies of the Spirit within all Christians to find our special calling and to follow it – in daily life, at home in the community, in the local church and in the wider world. United by one hope – 'one Lord, one faith, one baptism, one God, and father of all, who is above all and through all and in all' (Eph. 4.4).

Most churches would say now that they are committed to recognizing and valuing the vocation of all people. Your church may have travelled far down that road. There are signs that right across the Anglican Communion, Local Ministry or Total, Common Ministry or whatever title is used, is providing a practical strategy to harness all the energy for discovering the role and gifts of all God's people together in mission and ministry in the world. Here is a practical, imaginative book which will give your church members an opportunity to look again at what corporate leadership is required to support the ministries of clergy, readers, youth workers, laity in daily employment, and in the other lay ministries which are increasingly developing in church and community life. You will also be able to explore whether you see a need for more ordained ministries within a Ministry Leadership Team, to help build up the local church. Lastly you will find an emphasis on the need to ensure appropriate learning for everyone, and on the responsibility of the Diocese or Region to support and keep faith with you as you take new risks for the Kingdom of God.

I hope you will have much enjoyment and many rich rewards in exploring this handbook, and that it will play a significant part in discovering where the Holy Spirit is leading your church in company with others, in the joyful adventure of the Kingdom.

The Right Reverend John Perry
Bishop of Chelmsford

Making Use of this Handbook

This handbook invites you to take a new look at how you see God's gifts for mission distributed and put to use in and through your particular local church and its networks in the wider world. The core of the book offers three stages for corporate discussion, question and decision-making.

1 Your church now – where and why?

2 Where is God calling your church?

3 What leadership do you need?

The handbook recognizes and is designed to support many forms of collaborative ministry. In particular it suggests ways to review and strengthen the partnership of all church members in ministry and mission through the development of Ministry Leadership Teams. Three further stages offer detailed suggestions for:

4 Establishing a Ministry Leadership Team.

5 Keeping the Team healthy.

6 Ordained Local Ministry in the Team.

Two Basic Definitions to Get You Started

Local Ministry refers to the ways in which, increasingly all Christians, because of their commitment to Christ expressed in baptism, are sharing in the ministry that serves God's purposes through the whole church, in many differing ways.

Ministry Leadership Teams consist of those in ordained and licensed ministry and others who, together and in diversity, lead, encourage and build up the work of the whole Body of Christ.

Building on Your Strengths With Other Local Churches

Your church may already practise 'shared ministry' and see itself as a 'missionary congregation'. This book offers your entire congregation the opportunity to review where you are and to develop further. You are encouraged to invite as many people as possible locally to share responsibility for the kind of church you are becoming.

In workshops on developing collaborative local ministry three responses commonly recur:

1 'Oh yes, we've been doing this for 30 years – there's nothing new here.

2 'This is mind-blowing: how wonderful; what a chance for the church to find new confidence.

3 'Never in my life have I ever known a local church where any of this would make any sense.'

The assumption of this handbook is that inherited patterns of ministry in most churches, of whatever denomination, are severely off-balance. Familiar patterns often allow for a clerical displacement of the ministry of all God's people. The ideas and practical suggestions here are radical, literally, in that they merely look for the rudimentary conditions for any church to apply as a basis for its life and mission. A fundamental building block of any church is that everybody counts in the partnership of all their different roles and gifts. Effective co-operation in ministry for world and church is an essential precondition for Christian community.

Every time this book refers to your 'local church' you are asked to be aware of how – corporately and individually – you relate to all groups of people in your area and what partnership you have with neighbouring churches. If you do not already work with:

- the Baptists next door;

- a cluster of Anglican parishes locally;

- the Roman Catholic community;

- the United Reformed Church;

- the Salvation Army;

- the Methodists down the road;

- the Church you pass on the way to yours;

... why not start now?

This handbook arose as a means of forwarding the policy of the Anglican Diocese of Chelmsford, placing a strong emphasis on developing partnership in the ministry and mission of the whole people of God. In making it available now for use by any church there are bound to be some problems about use of words. For example, instead of bishop, priest, parish and PCC, Baptists would use leader, minister, church and church meeting.

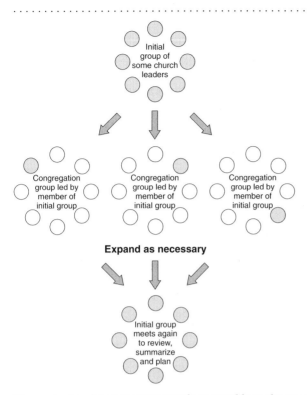

Figure 1 Involving as many people as possible in the process.

And behind the words used in various traditions lie differing emphases and meanings – not least of course within an Anglican setting.

To save constantly repeating different sets of terminology for each denomination, the handbook will keep its original Anglican framework by using the words bishop, priest and parish where these are being referred to quite specifically, but will normally use local church to refer to the worshipping congregation, and church council as a generic word to cover PCC, vestry or church meeting.

The handbook has been designed for a small but representative group of local church leaders (ordained and lay), initially to read through and decide how best to make use of it in any given situation. It is offered as a tool to stimulate creative and imaginative thinking in small groups with a concern to grow in mission and ministry. It is not a single-track route to a pre-planned destination. Figure 1 illustrates how small groups could be generated – depending on the numbers involved – to ensure that everyone with an interest can take part in these discussions. Members of the initial group can become leaders of other groups to work through the issues raised here. Experience shows that some stages will take several meetings, many months or years – but time spent now,

involving as many people as possible, will lay strong foundations for future developments. Minds and hearts need to be converted to the basic principle of local ministry –
through exploration, learning and celebrating Christ's faith and discipleship – before too
much thought is given to structures. Certainly, trying to develop new ministerial patterns
will flow more surely when preceded and surrounded by a deep engagement with God
and God's purposes in your location(s). Even for you to decide what is 'local' for a group
or cluster of church(es) may take long and honest discussion.

This handbook aims to bring together Tradition and tradition – the rich and complex
story of stories of 2,000 years of experiment in Christian community living and the
smaller-scale kaleidoscope of stories of every church in its particular location. Tradition
and tradition only make sense when they are seen in reciprocal communication. The
local and the catholic flourish best when held in dynamic tension.

This book contains a wide range of resources and discussion starters from which your
church can make choices. Be carefully selective. Some parts may seem more relevant to
you than others. Take what you need at this moment. Use complementary resources from
elsewhere and all your powers of imagination. If the issues here are truly identified and
engaged with, you will have to handle some creative conflict about what kind of church
you are to be. For ordained persons there are special anxieties: is my previous ministry
being criticized, do I have a place in a collaborative church, is priesthood being lost?
These are not reasons for ignoring the questions in this book, but a Christian community
will want to have a concern for all its members. Check to see who is lost or feeling
excluded – and why.

Preparation for group leaders and members

- Set aside time to familiarize yourself with the whole book.

- Prepare in advance for each session.

- Record key ideas or points discussed for later consideration.

- Be aware of and try to address what hinders some group members from participating
  fully.

- A highly recommended simple guide to groups is: Gaie Houston, *The Red Book of Groups
  and How to Lead Them Better.*

> 66 New Testament teaching about vocations has been rediscovered in the last thirty years by Christians
> of many different denominations. We can thank God that it is now strongly affirmed by many of the
> members of the Church of England. 99
> ALL ARE CALLED

This handbook is built on themes often explored in the international, ecumenical
thinking about God, Mission, Baptism, Eucharist and Ministry of the past 30 years or
so. It invites you to engage with the key ideas shaping our understanding of Christian
community identity:

- Christian faith as living God's life in the world (1 John 3.14–18).

- The purpose of the church as a community that is united, upheld by God's life, attending to the whole of life, and sharing God's passion for the transformation of all creation (John 17.21; 1 Cor. 1.24, 30–31, 10.32; 2 Cor. 1.2, 3–5, 9, 19–20, 21–22, 24; Eph. 1, 2.13–16, 4.31—5.2; 6.10).

- Ministry as a function of the church as a whole, not only the leaders, clerical and lay (Rom. 12.1; 1 Cor. 10—11 and 12; Heb.; 1 Pet. 1.13–17, 2.9–10; 2 Pet. 3.11–13; Rev. 1.6, 5.10).

- The need to discover and develop important new roles for ordained ministers, following the call of the Spirit to respond to the urgent needs of the present (1 Kings 18.21; Matt. 14.28–29; Acts 2.3; 11.1–18; 15.22, 28; 1 Cor. 2.9–10; Eph. 4.11–12).

- An emphasis on incarnation – ministering after the pattern of Jesus in the entire neighbourhood and the world of daily occupation, questioning every authority (Matt. 3.16–17, 4.8–10; 10.35–42; Mark 1.10, 22; Luke 3.22; 4.1, 16–21; John 8.28; 1 Cor. 12.28; 14.31–33; 2 Cor. 4.6; Gal. 2.20; Eph. 2.20; 3.14–21; 4.11; Heb. 4.14–15, 10).

- Each local church as an embodiment of the church in every age and every place (Rom. 12.4; 1 Cor. 12.12ff and 14; Eph. 2.8; 4.4–7 and 11–15; 6.11–18; Col. 1.18).

You will certainly want to add to this list.

This handbook assumes that parishes and local churches will for most Christians in Britain continue to develop over the first part of the third millennium through a theology and practice of mission earthed in the particulars of time and place. In the mobile society of today most people will draw their identity from belonging to a cluster of localities. For example, there are those who will be worshipping on a Sunday, working through the week and living in a home, all three of which are in separate locations with potentially conflicting allegiances. This complex situation often leads to a compartmentalization leading to a separation between where one lives, works and worships.

Further, every locality – of worship, work and home – is in fact increasingly experienced as diverse and possibly in conflict. A consequence of this will often be a refusal to make connections between those core places. A basic truth for all human beings is that we can only be in one place at a time. Crucially being in any one place always contains our God-given way of developing both as a human person and as one who through baptism and eucharist is constantly being drawn into the new possibilities that Christ has in store for us. Discovering more and more of what it means to say 'I turn to Christ', is to become more truly oneself as one growing in response both to Jesus Christ and to others.

A key purpose of this handbook is to consider the ministry of the local church no longer as the sole task of the ordained, nor as sometimes delegated by them to laity, but as a developing partnership in every aspect of the church's life and work – gathered and dispersed, local and regional – in the local church and diocese.

xv

> 66 And all of us, with unveiled faces, seeing the glory of the Lord, as though reflected in a mirror, are being transformed into the same image from one degree of glory to another; for this comes from the Lord, the Spirit. 99
> 2 COR. 3.18

Accumulated experience is showing that for shared ministry to become deeply rooted in the life of a church it must be embraced as a strategy not only locally but regionally and in every network ecumenically – in committees, boards, synods, budgets, education and training in seminary, courses and groups – as a partnership between all the different but equal ministries to which Christians are called in mission. The whole 'environment' created by regional church leaders has to 'give permission' for partnership ministry to be a low level, normal and also fundamental priority. The words of bishops, diocesan officers and others in synods and documents have to be backed up in consistent, reflective behaviour. To change the ministry paradigm will take sustained, persistent, everyday commitment.

> 66 There is no special status in the kingdom for those in 'top jobs' or with 'important responsibilities'. 99
> ALL ARE CALLED

This handbook is not offering a little scheme for keen churches. Rather it seeks to encourage the creation of a holistic policy that in every relationship in every local church, there is the partnership of all the baptized, in both difference and equality, in the Body of Christ, for God's Mission in the whole of the world. It assumes the belief that every local church is to see itself as a hologram of the whole church in time and space. A general concern to develop the ministry of laity is being focused in the movement some call 'local ministry'. Anglicans in Connecticut call this 'total common ministry'; in New Zealand it is called 'mutual ministry'; in Perth (Australia) they speak of 'becoming ministering communities'. The local church crucially needs the assurance of a wider environment that will support and help ministry as partnership flourish.

> 66 I will count you a kingdom of priests, a consecrated nation. 99
> EXOD. 19.3–8

The strength of this movement, in Britain increasingly called 'local ministry', is to:

- recognize and co-operate with God's presence and activity in the world, so that Christians are deliberately choosing to become co-workers for the Kingdom;
- expect all church members, because of their Baptism, to see themselves as part of the life and mission of the church in all its parts;

- build up and stimulate faith, gifts and responsibilities in the whole church;

- distribute properly the tasks of ministry throughout the entire membership of the church.

Many churches of all denominations have had local ministry teams by one name or another for years – for pastoral work, worship leading, teaching or faith development. In reality, though, some of these have been committees rather than ministering bodies.

In this handbook a Ministry Leadership Team (MLT) – in whatever different local form – is given the distinctive task of building up and distributing all the ministries of the worshipping and witnessing Body of Christ in God's world and church. Figure 6 illustrates how a MLT can help to focus or provide a gearing system for all kinds of ministry teams, depending on the size and complexity of your situation. In small churches the whole congregation may be the MLT.

The phrase 'Ministry Leadership Team' has been chosen because of its flexibility. Large or small, every church and every team can be part of the present ecumenical journey towards new patterns of mission and ministry.

There will always be different views on 'leadership' coloured by each person's own experiences. For those with a memory of the leadership of a highly directive person, who knows exactly where (s)he is driving a group, forcing them to take a predetermined route, there will be wariness of leadership. But Scripture and the best Christian practice inspired by God's Spirit and the life of Jesus Christ offer understandings of leadership rooted in mutual love as a vital and important part of the life of a local church. Like all human organizations, churches need leadership, but leadership that will be empowering and releasing for the entire congregation. This is not to say that collaborative (working-together) ministry does not allow particular people or roles sometimes to suggest, powerfully, a new direction to be tested by the whole community through its representatives. Experience of churches and other complex organizations today points to the requirement for leaders to have a wide repertoire of different styles to be deployed as necessary. A versatile and confident overall leader will allow for different people to take the lead as appropriate. As the Gloucester Diocese expresses it: 'Local Ministry Teams are for the prayerful, rooting, encouragement, enabling, drawing out, gentle restraining, focusing, nurturing of the whole congregation in its will for the Kingdom of God – a sign that God calls lay and ordained in partnership.' Leadership will need constant appraisal and, where necessary, reformation. Stage Three of this book offers the chance to examine the nature of Christian leadership in general as well as the particular needs for leadership in your local church.

All ministry teams, whatever their context, have a common underlying purpose – to help churches grow up and stand on their own feet with an awareness and appreciation of the richness of belonging to the wider church too.

So through a Ministry Leadership Team, including the clergy and other accredited ministers, working for a shared understanding and responsibility for 'what it means to be the church in our particular places' can be a continuing project. Specifically, Ministry Leadership Teams – in partnership with church councils:

- **grow** in shared prayerful discernment of the changing purposes, priorities and practical ministries of the local church;

- **study** together, using everyone's resources;

- **undertake** tasks and roles, within the team, according to gifts, needs, and availability;

- **encourage, challenge and draw out** the gifts and vocations of the whole church;

- **undertake and co-ordinate** the normal church-based ministries, in the light of the parish's mission;

- **support and develop** witness and ministry in the world of everyday occupations.

> 66 religions die when their light fails, that is when they lose their power to interpret convincingly the full range of present experience in the light of their idea of God. 99
> WOLFHART PANNENBERG

For decades we have had the rhetoric for collaborative ministry. Many churches have worked experimentally, often with effective results. Much still depends on who is the ordained minister in charge. The remark of Bishop John Robinson that no parish can get more excited than the vicar, still rings true. Local Ministry is a movement that offers to give renewed practical expression to partnership in ministry in a church rooted in a vision.

Local Ministry is everywhere different yet always about building up confidence together, so that the gifts of all can be released and used – in ministry within the church and mission in the whole world. It's about growing up and knowing our true power in the local church in partnership with diocese, region and world-wide church. It's about ordained and lay Christians sharing responsibility together for building the faith and confidence that will enable a church to be a truly dynamic presence in the wider community.

Neither Ministry Teams in general nor a Ministry Leadership Team in particular displace the ministries of others. They are to be agents of the development of everyone drawing gifts and vocations from among all church members. And because lay and ordained people increasingly share the leadership of the church, the team acts as a sign to the community that it is not 'the vicar' who is the church, but all of us, together.

This kind of transformation in ministry needs to go very deep, and certainly doesn't happen overnight. It requires the combination of excitement about who we could be as a church, and practical determination and an attitude of constant learning.

One Diocesan Local Ministry Officer writes:

What Ministry Leadership Teams typically do:

- The particular underlying role of a Ministry Leadership Team is to provide a way of focusing and distributing ministries. It's a role which can only be fulfilled by a team of lay and ordained working together, not by isolated individuals. Ministry Leadership Teams are typically chosen to lead, encourage, enable, draw out and build up the whole worshipping, witnessing Body of Christ locally. They do this by meeting together regularly to pray for, co-ordinate, and discern need and direction in ministry and mission locally.

- Particular ministries: Team members are usually also involved in, and sometimes lead or co-ordinate, specific areas of ministry. Some call these Local Ministry Teams – which depend on the priorities of the church and community locally. They work together with, and encourage, many other local people in developing and extending gifts and ministry through the church and in a wider world.

CAROLINE PASCOE

How Might a Ministry Leadership Team Work in Practice?

Just as the leadership and ministry of the early churches was amazingly varied, a Ministry Leadership Team could be set up in a huge variety of ways depending on which local church you belong to.

The following examples are offered to stimulate discussion on how local churches could develop local ministry in their situation.

Small market town and six villages

In a cluster of seven distinct neighbourhoods there are six Anglican parishes each with their church councils. Joan is the ordained minister for all these churches, based at St Mary's, and Tony is the reader. The six churches are each at different stages of development towards collaboration that recognizes the ministry of everyone. Joan is finding it increasingly difficult to meet local expectations about leading worship in all churches. Each church sees her on a Sunday only twice per month. She is also aware that the quality of pastoral care has declined since the churches were brought together five years ago, partly because a non-stipendiary minister who used to be licensed to the parishes has moved away. She suggests to each church council that it should consider establishing a Local Ministry Leadership Team. St Leonard's refuses to discuss the concept of Local Ministry, remaining firmly wedded to the practice of an ordained minister being sent to each church from outside. St James' feels unable to accept Local Ministry at present, but at St Mary's Joan, Tony, and some members of the council study the handbook together. At the end of long discussions involving most of the congregation the principles are understood and accepted. One year later, the council votes unanimously to move towards setting up a Ministry Leadership Team.

Eight names are suggested to be members of the team in training, of whom six are chosen through a discerning process. The team begins to work and to meet regularly for worship and training. Gradually the members begin to take more responsibility for worship and ministry in the parish so that, by the end of a year they are completely responsible for a monthly family service which has been added to the two services per month previously offered. During the year Joan and Tony have joined with the rest of the team for regular prayers, study and planning. Six months further on St James' Church Council, impressed by the developments at St Mary's, begins to study the handbook. The Bishop, who has been keeping closely in touch through a diocesan facilitator, recognizes and commissions the team.

Five years after it began its work and education, the Team is re-authorized by the Bishop. It is now responsible for the primary pastoral care of the parish, visiting each person on the electoral roll twice each year and every other house annually. The Team plans and leads a monthly family service, and during each of the last three Easter holidays has organized a children's holiday club with the encouragement of the Diocesan Children's Officer. The Team is now also responsible for a monthly Sunday Eucharist which is celebrated by a recently ordained NSM, so now the parish has a weekly service instead of fortnightly. The incumbent is still present at two services per month as she was five years earlier. The Team has also decided to have a weekly evening Eucharist at which the NSM presides, and the attendance at this is slowly growing. One member of the Team has been elected on to the Parish Council and another has become chair of the village hall management committee. They both consider these developments to be a natural part of their membership of the Ministry Leadership Team.

Dormitory village

The parish of All Saints was a village on the edge of a large town, but due to an increasing number of houses being built in the last twenty years, it now has a population approaching 15,000. One of the largest employers in the country is situated within the parish. Together with Philip, the Vicar, are Margaret the Reader, and two assistant clergy – Anne in her second year of full-time ministry after ordination, and Peter who is an accountant and has been ordained (NSM) for five years.

There is a small church in a nearby hamlet within the parish.

A further major development is now taking place on the edge of the parish, and the PCC and Philip are concerned about how they can offer adequate pastoral care to the area and how they can symbolize the presence of the church within this new community. The major industry is sited on the same side of the parish as the new development, and for some time the parish has been discussing how it can relate to this employer. The PCC decides to explore local ministry and suggests the possibility of developing a Ministry Leadership Team with a two-fold purpose – first to be responsible for primary Christian ministry to the new development, and also to try to develop the church's presence in the local industry.

The Bishop recognizes that the team has two primary foci to its ministry, but that members may also be available more generally within the parish. A Team of eight people is established, and at the same time the new housing development is gradually being occupied. Three members of the Team recruit groups from the congregation to visit each house as people move in. Soon they begin a weekday carer and toddler club, and the Vicar celebrates the Holy Communion fortnightly in the house of a Team member who lives close to the new development. One member of the Team is a manager in the local industry. He finds that those responsible for making decisions about redundancy often approach him as a confidential listener, for they are aware of his role within the Ministry Leadership Team. He starts an informal support group during lunch hour for managers who feel that difficult decisions are causing them stress.

It is now two years since the Team began its work and learning together. They have begun fortnightly family services in the community hall on the new development, and they lead weekly prayer groups and bible studies. Two members of the group and Margaret the Reader with the advice and training of the Diocesan Youth Officer, begin an open youth club for young people from the new development.

Because there is a high degree of mobility in this area, after five years two of the original Team leave and two people from the new development take their place. The team works on the integration of new members into the Team, and the whole Team review some of their earlier learning for the benefit of new members.

Urban parish with three worship centres

St George's is a single parish with three churches. Rosemary the incumbent is due to retire in five years' time, and it is likely that the benefice will be combined with a neighbouring parish which has two churches. The Archdeacon suggests to the PCC that they ought seriously to consider local ministry as a way forward. After discussion they decide to explore. They really feel that their primary need is for an ordained person or persons, but they understand the reasons for the creation of a Ministry Leadership Team. The benefice undertakes to study the Resource Book with facilitators. The Team begins work and training. The Bishop authorizes the MLT and, a year later, two vocations to NSM emerge. Three years further on, Rosemary retires and the parish is amalgamated with a neighbouring benefice. The new incumbent, Chris, now has responsibility for five churches, and celebrates the Eucharist monthly in each of the churches and the NSMs and the Team ensure that each church has a weekly service. The Team devises a family service each month, which it leads with slight alterations in each of the churches in turn. The NSMs each celebrate the Eucharist twice per month on Sundays, and once each mid-week. Another member of the parish, Mike, has begun training as a Reader on the diocesan course, and is being integrated into the Team.

Members of the Team are increasingly involved in developing the Church's ministry in the wider community. They are taking a leading part in establishing a voluntary transport scheme for those without access to cars; a self-help group for single parents has been set up; and there is an old-people's lunch club in a Church Hall.

Market town parish

St Cuthbert's is a well-supported church with vigorous and dynamic leadership sacrificially offered by Eric the incumbent, who has ministered to the needs of the parish for fifteen years. He is renowned for being a charismatic preacher, and over the years has nurtured the congregation well so that many people have discovered and exercised gifts in themselves which were previously lying dormant. The ancient pews are packed for all three Sunday Services and the music group is the envy of other churches. There is a network of lay-led Bible Study Groups and an established Good Neighbour Scheme. Children's work thrives and old people are visited regularly.

People often comment to his wife how amazed they are that the Vicar never seems to stand still for five minutes, and they wonder how he manages to go on attending every single meeting and to keep such a finger on the pulse of everything that goes on. He really is a marvel! His wife smiles weakly and acknowledges their accolades, secretly wishing her husband would find time to learn to share some of the huge parish responsibilities he has held onto so firmly for so long. Some people in the congregation have tried to prise open his grip, but the Vicar has always seen his role as being the sole decision-maker and the controller of all that goes on under the church banner.

Eventually, however, Eric is persuaded to take the advice of his longstanding spiritual director and to attend an Area Conference with his two churchwardens and another concerned lay person, to consider a fresh model of how a Church might grow up into the full stature of Christ. Eric silently breathes a sigh of relief when he glimpses the wider possibilities a Ministry Leadership Team might allow for the life and mission of St Cuthbert's, including the benefit of freeing his energy to explore other still undiscovered gifts of ministry in himself.

Eric takes a well-earned day off at last and the congregation celebrates its coming of age.

Could your church already write a similar story?

What could the story of your church be like in two or three years – taking seriously the vision and practice of Local Ministry in your location? How many stories need to be told from different perspectives to understand the whole? Why not ask several people to attempt this story writing in your local church and then to reflect on the differing styles, emphases and blind spots in several accounts? You may prefer to use a tape recorder or some other way of presenting your stories. Could it be strengthened through clustering with others of the same or a different denomination? What will be the challenges and opportunities of setting up a Ministry Leadership Team in an ecumenical setting?

A final word about using this handbook. There will inevitably be some ideas or expressions that are unhelpful or puzzling. Rather than allowing this to become a reason for rejecting the whole project, remember that it is offered in humility: as a set of questions to pursue the development of thinking and action in your location. In the end all the language, forms of ministry and understandings of a local church have to be owned by those directly involved. But is it possible to be a Christian church when the local chooses to be disconnected from the issues and questions raised by Christian churches in other ages and locations?

Take your time. Be content to work slowly. There is no fast solution in Local Ministry. Bishop Edward King reminds us that we should respect others, their difficulties, their wishes, their feelings, their habits – even their unreasonable prejudices.

Your Church Now – Where and Why?

Together take an honest look at your church(es) – in all the ways in which you are presently attempting to serve God's purposes in the world, your local neighbourhood and congregation. Begin with the positives.

Celebrating What You Are Proud Of

Take stock, reflect, discuss among yourselves ... What you are justly proud of, what gifts have you received, where are you healthy and can say 'truly God is in this place'?

St Paul says we should not be ashamed of the Gospel (Rom. 9.33, 10.11). Whether we like it or not, the general public judge our 'good news' by the quality of our church

66 God is greater than our hearts and he knows everything ... by this we know that we abide in him and he in us, because he has given us of his Spirit ... God is love, and those who abide in love abide in God, and God abides in them. 99
1 JOHN 4

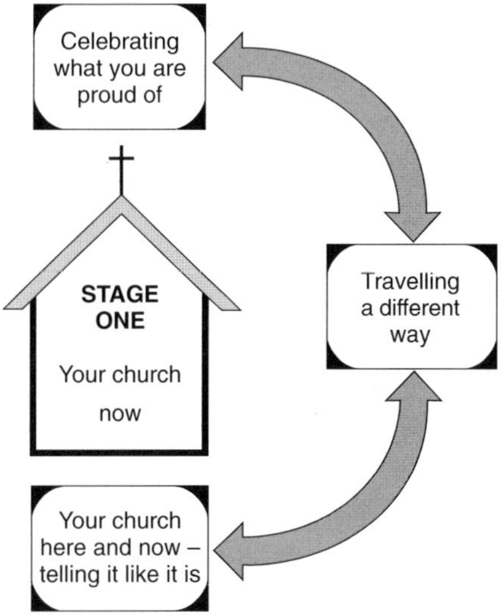

Figure 2

life and so assess our belief. As a demonstration of what we really believe – about God, ourselves, society and the world – our church practice is an open book for all to read. So it follows we need to be able to be proud of the way we deliberately choose to be the church.

In recent decades, churches have been developing partnerships between ordained and lay Christians in specific areas of mission and ministry.

What does your church have to celebrate about the following? The points are arranged alphabetically. You could draw a diagram to show their relative significance in your church now. Note the range of views in your group and how much weight is given to each.

- administration
- bible study groups
- caring for buildings as a sign of God's presence
- children's work
- being together at home
- development of lay ministries
- ecumenical partnership
- evangelism

- faith development
- home groups
- involvement of young people in leadership
- involvement with children
- links with statutory bodies
- links with other faith communities
- marriage preparation
- ministries in the workplace
- music ministry

- outreach parenting courses
- partnership with local neighbourhood groups
- pastoral care – visiting
- prayer groups – intercession, contemplation

- publicity

- social action – in neighbourhood or globally

- spiritual direction – soul friending

- study – reflection on faith and life

- support for everyday occupations

- training for ministries

- witnessing

- youth activities

- work with young people

- world church links

- worship – preparation for leadership.

It's so easy to get bogged down in detail, discouragement and the sheer pressure of apparently what 'has' to be done. We can all see the causes for penitence now and in the church's past, but don't forget also to be positive and celebrate the good.

Involve the whole church through an exhibition or display and an act of worship to celebrate what has been and continues to be worth celebrating about your church.

> 66 When Exodus tells us that God's true name is, I AM, we are reminded that ultimate reality is always just here, right now. 99
> EXOD. 3.14

> 66 The church is a community of desire for the feast of the Kingdom of God, and joy is at the heart of that desire. 99
> DAVID FORD

Your Church Here and Now – Telling it Like it is

What type of Church are you?

The following 'models' of church are sometimes spoken of. In the group consider which dimensions are strongest in your situation and look for examples of each in your local church. You may well wish to add further models to better describe your church's situation.

- **The Institution**: we are part of the earthly institution, rooted in Scripture, tradition and reasoning, that has Christ's authority to teach and sanctify.

- **The Parish Church**: we are here for all who work or live in the neighbourhood – unless they opt out.

3

- **The Mystical Communion**: we are Christ's body growing into perfection helping us to bring in the Kingdom of God.

- **The Sacrament**: we are the visible sign to the human race of God's grace in Christ.

- **Healing Community**: we are expecting and often experiencing the resurrection power of Jesus Christ to transform our personal lives and the networks to which we belong.

- **The Reconciler**: we are working for justice and peace.

- **The Herald**: we are those who have an authority to preach the divine message of the gospel to the world.

- **The Servant**: we are here to serve the world and each other.

- **The Congregation**: we are God's people, responsible to one another before God.

What really matters to your Church?

Describe this key question, relating to such issues as:

- What are we here for?

- Why spend all this energy, time and money doing what we do?

- What parts of the story and teaching of Jesus best fit with our way of being a church?

On a large sheet of paper, in no more than 20 words complete this section:

On present evidence, the mission of our church is:

One way to achieve this is to ask people to work first on their personal answer, then in pairs, in fours and gradually through conversation, arrive at a consensus. But tell it 'as it is' – not as you would like it to be. You may have to accept that you have several answers that cannot be reconciled.

66 Learning is not the main thing in life – it is the only thing. 99
PETER HONEY

66Then afterward I will pour out my spirit on all flesh, your sons and daughters shall prophesy, your old men shall dream dreams. 99
JOEL 2.28–29

Make a list of all that could be called 'outreach' in your current church life and ask who is responsible for each item.

1

2

3

4

Listening to all the groups that have met, this could be written up as a large poster in your church and in your church magazine.

How ecumenical are you?

Ask yourselves how committed you are to the unity of the church. What practical form do you think this unity should eventually take in your locality? How open are you to working with neighbouring churches – or those of other denominations? Spend some time honestly facing these questions using this check list:

- **Ecumenical Lent group.**
- **Common marriage preparation.**
- **Ecumenically organized pastoral care.**
- **Joint worship.**
- **Joint learning, e.g. bible study.**
- **Bereavement counselling.**
- **Ecumenical youth groups.**
- **Joint training for junior church leaders.**
- **Joint evangelism.**
- **Joint baptism preparation.**

Discipleship and ministry

Ministry in churches is going through a major transformation with many prophetic experiments and a wide variety of understandings being given voice. In many churches now 'shared' ministry is the norm where laity 'help' in many areas of church life previously considered the territory of clergy.

66 Joy is the power of telling our own stories. 99
ANN LEONARD

66 The purpose of God according to Holy Scripture is to gather the whole of creation under the lordship of Christ Jesus in whom, by the power of the Holy Spirit, all are brought into communion with God. 99
ROM. 8.21 AND EPH. 1

66 as forgiven betrayers. 99
MARK 14.17–19

> 66 commissioned through grace. 99
>
> LUKE 5.8

> 66 disturbing visions from God. 99
>
> ACTS 10

> 66 Paul's conversion. 99
>
> ACTS 9.1–22

> 66 Change is possible but it must start with self-acceptance. 99
>
> ALEXANDER LOWEN

> 66 Instead of using only revelation and tradition as starting points ... we must start with facts and questions derived from the world and from history. 99
>
> GUSTAVO GUTIERREZ

> 66 It's not the Church of God which has a mission, it's the God of Mission who has a Church. 99
>
> TIM DEARBORNE

> 66 Seek the welfare of the city where I have sent you into exile, and pray to the Lord on its behalf ... 99
>
> JER. 29.7

What differences do you see between discipleship and ministry? What are the characteristics of every follower of Jesus Christ as the background for particular callings?

In discussion together, complete the following sentences, consulting the scriptures as you feel appropriate. Write your conclusions on a flip chart or large piece of paper which all can see.

- Discipleship is ...

- Ministry is ...

Explore where discipleship or ministry is at work:

- in the church's 'gathered' life of worship, community and outreach;

- in the church's 'dispersed' life of all its members every-day.

All churches that are alive have informal networks of caring and praying for those in need – locally and globally. Does your church have any formal scheme for lay ministries? How does it operate?

How did these 'ministers' get their role?

What initial and regular training and support for ministry development has been available/taken-up locally or at a wider level?

To summarize your findings, draw a poster-size diagram that shows:

- Who ministers to whom in the local church and neighbourhood.

- The points of contact between your church and neighbourhood.

- Where the responsibilities are held.

- Ecumenical links.

- Links with other faith communities.

Travelling a Different Way

Listening to the needs of the world and your local area

Considering all ministry as partnership raises questions about which other organizations in the neighbourhood the local church is or could be working with.

Christian ministry is the way the church shapes its full co-operation with all of God's work in the world. All people have the task of discerning for themselves, and with others, what God is doing in their lives and in society and the world at large. Christians believe that takes place within a world which is already redeemed by Christ. In all the strands of daily life, God calls us to be interpreters and co-workers. Precisely what is 'local' is a growing question – members of the group may occupy a range of very different territories throughout the week. Many groups in a different neighbourhood all bring different and overlapping interpretations of what matters and what is happening to them.

Undertake a simple survey in your area covering whatever questions seem most relevant, e.g. age groups, institutions, schools, colleges, variety of ethnic origins, different faith communities, levels of unemployment, types of work available, housing types, levels of stressful occupation, provisioning of social services and levels of prosperity.

Especially try to hear the voice of minorities or those on the 'edge' of your local community. Ask how your local issues relate to the wider world scene.

Keep it simple. Local authorities and voluntary agencies may already hold information to help you listen to what the needs are and to begin to respond. Look out for new publications from your borough or local council. There may be people willing to take a roving microphone into shopping areas to get short comments from local people. Or you could make a short video or photographic exhibition. Don't forget to look for the unexpected and often invisible parts of your area.

Looking at the information you gather, ask 'So what?'

- How much of this information is new to you – what do you make of it? What are people going through? What questions are people asking?

- What do you think are the most significant relationships? Why? How are they sustained or neglected?

- What do people want most? Why?

- What are the root causes of how things are now?

> 66 The missionary journey is, for the Christian, both a journey in and a journey out ... The kingdom 'within' and the kingdom 'without' are two aspects of one journey. 99
> DAVID CLARK

> 66 Paul seemed to be motivated, not simply as the result of personal call, but by the discovery of the presence of the risen Christ in the world itself ... so much so that travelling was for him a constant finding of Christ. 99
> DANIEL W. HARDY

> 66 It is this world that is being redeemed. 99
> ROM. 8.19–21

> 66 The Kingdom agenda includes everything. 99
> REV. 21–26

THE MINISTRY TEAM HANDBOOK

66 Only when the church identifies itself with the poor and oppressed can it accomplish its prophetic function. 99
ENRIQUE DUSSEL

66 Sometimes I've believed as many as six impossible things before breakfast. 99
LEWIS CARROLL

MATT. 2.12

66 It is the people of Israel who are saved, publicly and communally. 99
EXOD. 12—50

- Which are the agencies of change and of building up the neighbourhood? How is change actually happening? Find out and make a display of where individual members of your church are already involved as workers or volunteers in the neighbourhood. Draw a diagram that shows all the links between church and wider communities.

- What still needs transforming in the neighbourhood and the places where you work and the wider world?

- How is the church as such showing solidarity and involvement with the needs of local people?

- How could this co-operation be further developed? Who will take an initiative, and when?

Living in a world of rapid change

To set the life of your church in the context of working for God's Kingdom, look at change as it now affects the world at large. Choosing examples from this list – or from a range of today's newspapers – discuss such fundamental possibilities as:

- **Alterations to life as we know it** – euthanasia, genetic engineering, termination of pregnancy.

- **Changes in human relating** – marriage, race, sexuality.

- **Religious and cultural pluralism** – living alongside people of different faiths and ways of life.

- **Particular pressures on the young** – drug abuse, changing nature of employment, education anxieties, ethnic minorities.

- **The increasing pace of life** – advantages and pressures of computers, instant communications, high-speed travel.

- **Cosmic issues** – global warming, destruction of rain forests, international debt, nuclear weapons.

Discussion prompts

- What are the issues that really matter to you?

- Why do they matter so much?

- How would you like to see change happen?

- Who has power in these situations?

How open to moving on are you?

Throughout this stage, you are looking basically at 'How things are' – the positives and the negatives in your locality and church. You have hopefully recorded your pleasure at many good things in the life of your church. Are you ready now to face up to some dissatisfaction as well? Be as forward looking as you dare.

In Stage Two of this handbook you will be invited to make decisions about real practical changes. Only as you consult locally will you know what they should be. There may seem to be an impossible gulf between how you are and how you feel God is calling for transformation.

Human communities don't operate well when faced with lists of 'shoulds' and 'oughts'. There are bound to be disagreements among you. How can you prepare for this?

There is a vital creative link which will help you to move on, in a way that is not forced. Enquire – as honestly as you can – what are the roles, influences and relationships in your church life which will make all the difference to whether change is easy or difficult. Some roles are key, and can be occupied in a forward-looking and open way, or more concerned with the past, and closed.

- What has been your church's past history of mission and ministry?

- Is there anything that has become fossilized about your church's life?

- Do your own personal attitudes and influence help with the forward planning of your church?

- As you do this in the group, try to see the distinction between persons and the roles they occupy within the everyday working of the parish, e.g. treasurers, clergy, flower arrangers, musicians, children's workers, churchwardens, administrators, readers, house-group leaders, pastoral visitors, educators and sidepersons.

- Try drawing some diagrams to make your situation clearer – you could enjoy yourselves as you struggle

66 Sometimes I get lonesome for a storm. A full-blown storm where everything changes. 99
JOAN BAEZ

66 We must pray not just for the poor and unfortunate but with them. If we pray 'in his spirit' we can afford to be despised by those who consider themselves intelligent and enlightened; but not by those who are disconsolate, suffering or oppressed. 99
J. B. METZ

66 We do not appropriate Christ for our use. We do not change him, but he changes us. We do not grasp him but he grasps us. 99
JÜRGEN MOLTMANN

66 God fills everything in every way. 99
EPH. 1.23

9

> 66 Abram went as the Lord had told him. 99
> GEN. 12.1–9

> 66 New birth is painful but reveals God's glory. 99
> ISA. 66.5–13

> 66 'your Kingdom come, your will be done, on earth as in heaven.' 99
> MATT. 6.10

> 66 'Follow me.' 99
> LUKE 5.27

> 66 Change is hard for those with much at stake. 99
> JOHN 6.66

> 66 truth, nobility, integrity, justice, purity, beauty. These are the marks of full well-being as this is found in God, and they are found in the world only because they arise there from the fullness of God. 99
> DANIEL W. HARDY

> 66 From the rising of the sun to its setting, my name is great among the nations, says the Lord. 99
> MAL. 1.11

to agree, and perhaps find laughter as a way round possible difficulties.

- Where are the strengths, weaknesses, and opportunities for the healthy development of your church?

Check out the assumptions behind the following phrases

'We've always done it like this.'

'We tried that 20 years ago and it didn't work.'

'In my last parish, my wardens and my organist were a great help to my ministry.'

'Our Rector gives a lot of freedom to the laity.'

'That's what we pay the vicar for.'

'Nobody round here will do anything but me.'

'If you want a job done properly, do it yourself.'

Remember these issues as you consider – and let the results shape your future planning:

- work to get clear about your goal;

- involve all 'leaders' from the start;

- involve every person who will join in;

- agree on a method, timescale, required skills;

- knowing that so many people's lives are already heavily loaded, negotiate how much time and energy each person can realistically offer – it will vary depending on other responsibilities;

- use symbols and pictures as well as words in vision forming;

- keep everyone informed of meetings and documents;

- integrate discussion with prayer;

- listen to all voices – some who speak from the margin are prophetic;

- recognize that between the old and the new there will be uncertainty and ambiguity – look after one another on the way.

STAGE TWO

Where is God Calling Your Church?

Stage One gave you the opportunity to find out about the setting of your church and the realities as you see them now, and to consider where change is needed. In this next stage you are urged to let your imaginations soar. Co-operating with God for the Kingdom, how do you see your church's developing purpose in mission and ministry?

What kind of church you are called to be is a crucial question. What is at stake is the truth about God, which cannot be separated from the situation in which you find yourself, and the identity and mission of your faith community. In the next three or five years what do you hope for and what are you prepared to work for, through God's grace?

❝ In their relationships and actions of care, social change, adult formation, worship and stewardship, communities of faith enact their core values of human being, truth, destiny, knowledge and obligation. **❞**
ELAINE GRAHAM

Letting the Trinity Shape You

How we relate to one another and to the world as church can be transformed when we allow our community of faith to be rooted in God, three persons in community, the creating and saving work of the Trinity. This section invites you to make fruitful connections between your church practice and God's life with us experienced as an overflowing community of diversity in unity.

Christian experiences of God's life

All our talk of the divine mystery is partial. There are as many ways as there are experiences – and God eludes them all. But people of faith usually want to struggle to find analogies from everyday speech that at least give hints of how they have known something of God's reality. Luke 2.19 and 51 illustrate the way our understanding can grow through the study and contemplation of believers, treasuring these things in their hearts. From

❝ All the elements in the circle of God's life in the world have a certain role to play; and yet they are deeply reliant on each other. More than that, they must learn how to animate each other: each to lift the others: the life of God lifting the world by means of the church. The life of God lifting the church by means of all who are baptized, who are themselves stimulated by a faithful education and leadership to appreciate ever more fully the life to God in the world. **❞**
DANIEL W. HARDY

11

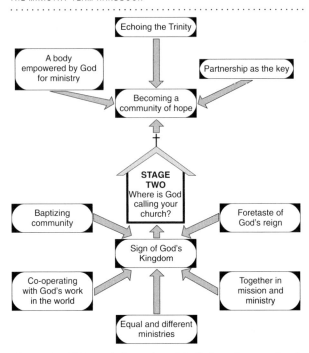

Figure 3. Taking a holistic view of God's hope for your church.

the start Christians began to think of God as more like a community than an isolated person, a fellowship held together by love and sharing. This picture of God as loving community is not a selfish one but one that overflows in open and generous relationship with all creation. There is not a worked out doctrine of the Trinity in the New Testament – it took several centuries of worship and thought for Christians to put trinitarian thought into the words we use in creeds and prayer – and that work will never be finally over. But we can see traces of a trinitarian understanding of God in scripture, e.g. John 10.8, 14.13, 16 and 26 and John 16.12–15. Paul's blessing in 1 Thess. 5.23 delineates the Trinity very clearly. Our talking of God will always be a pale shadow of the divine mystery, a reflection of all we know and do not yet know of the living mystery we call God.

In the group, recall words from scripture and also hymns, songs, pictures and prayers that speak of the

Trinity, and discuss what it means for human living, speaking and relationships when God is known as triune. Look for connections in what you know of science, art, music, ecology, cosmology and other disciplines in which members of the group may have expertise. There may well be members of the group who have studied these connected issues already. Challenge them to contribute from what they have learned in ways that make connections with everyone else. On the interaction of scientific and theological thinking about ultimate reality see the writings of John Polkinghorne.

Look at and use some modern worship texts that explore these themes:

Father you give us life, Jesus you give us love,
Spirit you give wisdom, Holy Three you give us yourself.
Help us, O Holy One, To give our lives,
To give our love, To give our minds to you
David Adam

Praise the Maker, Son and Spirit,
One God in community,
Calling Christians to embody
Oneness and diversity.
Thus the world shall yet believe, when
Shown Christ's vibrant unity
Wild Goose Worship Group

Christianity is at heart about relationality and about community. Our relationship to God and with our neighbour cannot be separated. Salvation experienced as having a healed relationship with God is demonstrated in patterns of relationships with people and creation. *Koinonia* (community, communion, communication) is the proper character of churches that echo the patterns of God's own life.

Reflect together on what it would mean if your church had a vision where Luke 1.52 was a key to all relating:

- The last shall be first.

- The excluded ones shall be included.

- The mighty shall be put off their thrones.

66 Let us dream of a church in which Jesus is the very Word, our window into the Father's heart, in which the Spirit is not a party symbol. 99
WESLEY FRENSDORFF

66 A church rooted in the Trinity and founded for the Kingdom, should be a blazing example of the learning community. 99
DAVID CLARK

JOHN 14.17; 1 JOHN 1.2–10; 2 PET. 1.4; 1 COR. 1.9; 2 COR. 13.13; 1 JOHN 4.16; ROM. 6; 1 COR. 13; HEB. 13

66 (not just about the church, but concerning the whole created order) 99
REV. 21.1–4

13

ISA. 35.1–2, 5–7, 45.18–19, 61.1–2; PS. 113.7–9; PS. 119.43–8

• The humble shall be exalted.

How could you create a church community rooted in the Trinity with relations of:

• mutuality

• co-dependency

• love

• justice

as the key to everything you do?

Witness of the Early Church

The life that uniquely the God of Israel offered to the world was one of ordered mutuality, hope for the future, freedom from all that binds, and interdependent caring. This picture of God's work in the world is offered as a powerful yet untidy witness through tales and songs and poems and liturgies of the life of Israel. The New Testament does not show God as a hierarchy of Father–Son–Spirit, but as a dynamic interdependent, interweaving of various patterns of saving activity. Jesus of Nazareth showed us what God's love is like – sharing our human life, loving at immense cost (John 3.16). In Jesus, Christians believe God is at work, building up community, drawing the lost back into relationship. To explore this further:

• Read Philippians 2.7 – Jesus as slave with the rejected.

• Look for, list and discuss other New Testament passages that show Jesus working with compassion for wholeness, health and restoration.

• Reflect on Jesus' way of eating and drinking with outcasts (e.g. Luke 5.27–32).

• Read Matthew 14.16, where many of these themes come together (in Greek our English word 'compassion' means 'to feel in the guts together').

• Look at how bad distribution of wealth impedes relationship with God (Mark 10.17–31; Luke 16.19–31). The gospel of the Kingdom invites us to participate in God's life, through full community with others.

- Read Ephesians 2.13–22 – on the cross Jesus breaks down dividing walls and builds the household of God.

- In Hebrews 13.12–13 Jesus invites us to join him in sharing life with the despised and rejected.

- The Spirit is the power of the New Creation and brings all to new birth (John 17.21; Rom. 8.23; 2 Cor. 1.22; Eph. 2.18; Rev. 1.6).

66 (The church as salt and light.) 99
MATT. 5.13, 14

Consider that the Christian belief in the equality of worth of all people has its roots in the creation stories of Genesis and the saved and pilgrim people of Exodus. At the heart of this pilgrim people, this nomadic city, is worship of the living God – the celebration of who we are with God and with one another.

Bible study – Ephesians 4.7–17

Within the New Testament there are several key passages which prescribe the purpose of ministry with the church. One such is Ephesians 4.7–17. Please read it now.

66The trinitarian profession of faith is therefore not only the summation of the revelation of the mystery of God; it is also the concrete expression of the hiddeness of God, which is the origins, goal and essential content of all revelation. 99
WALTER KASPAR

A body empowered by God for ministry

There are many ways into understanding more deeply the mutuality of the members of the body of Christ. These notes are to help you read and meditate together on Ephesians 4. Use whatever other resources are helpful to understand this passage.

Ministry, mission and spirituality are slippery words. Each can be 'greedy', trying to absorb everything else, and none yield happily to neat watertight definitions.

One body

If ministry is what baptized believers do in response to their faith in Jesus Christ, mission is concerned with bringing the values and principles of his Kingdom to bear in situations where they are absent or under-developed. Spirituality provides the link between the two. Robert Warren defines spirituality as 'our under-standing and experience of how encounter with God takes place and how such an encounter is sustained'.

66 The world will come to believe not because of the clarity of our doctrinal formulations (important as this is) but because of the quality of our life as a loving, reconciling inclusive community in Christ. 99
J. CRAWFORD AND M. KINNAMON

Equal and different

At the beginning of Ephesians 4 we are reminded that all believers are part of one body (v 4); that all have received gifts (v 7,8) and are called to 'works of service (ministry) (v 12). Our gifts are to equip us for ministry. But our ministries are also gifts (v 11) – we neither earn nor own them, they belong to God and are given to us through our relationship with him.

The gifts and ministries that God gives to his people are equal in value, but different in nature. Some are to be teachers or leaders or carers of other believers, so that we can all function properly in our own ministries (v 11, 12). The majority are called to minister outside the church for the benefit of the world at large. All believers are to be built up into effective ministers in becoming all that the body of Christ is meant to (v 12, 13).

In pairs, then afterwards in the Group, share your understanding and response to Ephesians 4. Write up your findings on a flip chart or a large sheet of paper which all can see.

66 Local Ministry is 'about the focus of Christian community life together being more than the worshipping community, but about the whole of human life in a particular place'. Saying that the work of clergy and laity is correlative, equal but different and this is how they might relate to one another in effective units of mission in the local church. 99
DANIEL W. HARDY

66 A learning organization is one which facilitates the learning of all its members and consciously transforms itself and its context. 99
PEDLER, BURGOYNE AND BOYDELL

Partnership as the key

Ministry as partnership is not merely an option for churches, but essential if we are to be true to the God who calls us. The way we work must reflect God's own work and character.

Bear each of the following in mind as you ask God's guidance for your church's future:

1 A hesitant movement away from hierarchy towards a more mutual responsibility.

2 A more focused sense of purpose – an end in view, working with the timeless rhythm of the seasons.

3 A holistic, whole of life approach, embracing the personal, the neighbourhood, the institutional, communal and wider world.

4 Awareness that we are all both teachers and learners.

5 The need for new leadership roles and skills.

6 The possibility of not perpetuating traditional practices, but rather to be surprised, to ask questions and be capable of rapid and continuous change.

7 To allow for all parts of a neighbourhood or church to impact on each other and to notice where redesign becomes necessary.

66 where people continually expand their capacity to create the results they truly desire, where new and expansive patterns of thinking are nurtured, where collective aspiration is set free, and where people are continually learning how to learn together. 99
PETER SENGE

God's words of encouragement to your church
A Group on a parish weekend put their vision something like this:

Dear People of God in this congregation,

It has come to our notice that you have many talents including:

1 PET. 2.4

- the ability to praise with all kinds of music;

- the ability to worship through silence;

- the ability to share love through touch and words and action;

1 COR. 10.17; 2 COR. 1.6–7; 1 JOHN 1.3

- the ability to expound your faith through dance and drama;

- the ability to encounter each other through intellectual exchange;

- the ability to listen actively;

- the ability to teach and heal;

- the ability to paint and draw, to sew and knit and to sculpt in our presence.

We hereby authorize you, in loving co-operation with your parish priest, to assist in the worship and mission of your church, making full use of the aforesaid talents.

Yours affectionately

God – Creator, Redeemer, Sustainer.

What would your letter from God be saying about the practice of all ministries in and related to your church? Try drafting it together.

66 The invitation is about participation, not mere observation. We are not journeying in the universe but with the universe. We are not concerned about living in an evolving world but co-evolving with our world. We are parts of a whole, much greater than the sum of parts, and yet within each part we are interconnected with the whole. 99
DIARMUID O'MURCHU

The Trinity – challenging and changing how we are the Church

Now that you have studied this section, make a diagram together on a large sheet of paper. Show what are the shape, characteristics and values of a church living a trinitarian life; and also some practical implications about the quality of its relatedness with all.

66 Ultimately it is a complex of conditioned emotions which the individual feels towards the surrounding world and his fellows … it is to human beings and their feelings, sentiments, reactions, that all look for the fundamental roots of the community. 99
DAVID CLARK

As you do this exercise bear in mind especially how God's life can be shown in:

- communication between adult and child, those of differing race or culture or education;

- the distribution of responsibilities;

- structures and institutional life;

- forms of leadership;

- relations with those of other faiths;

- companionship with neighbourhood groups;

- relations with partner churches.

Sign of God's Kingdom

EZEK. 36.25–7; MARK 8.34–8; JOHN 3.1–16; JOHN 20.1–10; 1 JOHN 2.29; ROM. 6.1–11

Church as a baptizing community

Through baptism and Eucharist Christians are drawn into the life of the Trinity and into solidarity with one another and the whole world. The church is called in every place to be offering the world a working pattern of a new way of being. In the diocese now many parishes are preparing children to receive communion simply on the basis of their baptism. All who are part of the ministering body need to receive the nourishing of the Eucharist.

In the group explore the meaning of baptism using four interlocking themes:

GEN. 9.8–17, 17.1–8; EXOD. 6.2–9

- **Death and Resurrection:** read through the baptism service reflecting on references to being buried with Christ in his death, sharing in his being raised by the Father, and being reborn in the Spirit. Discuss how conversion, acceptance, forgiveness, growth and gifts of the Spirit flow around the themes of death and new life. What could this mean for you?

18

- **Bound to God and to one another:** new birth in Christ gives us the freedom from self-centredness that God promises. We practise this and grow in maturity through membership of the Body of Christ, the Christian Community. Read and discuss Romans 6.3–11. We belong to a complex pattern of families and communities. How can belonging to Christ and the church make a difference to all the other connections we have?

66 Christian vocation is to make the church into a deepening spiral of ever greater participation in the work of God in the world now. 99
DANIEL W. HARDY

- **Commissioning:** we are members of Christ and of his people, but we are also sent out in service to the world, sometimes together, often alone. Signed by Christ as his possession and under his protection, we are called to use the Spirit's gifts for God's purposes. In some churches baptismal candidates are anointed with oil to remind them that they are set apart for God's work. In the group, explore what each person's calling has been and what it might become. Are there phrases in the initiation services that draw out the aspect of commissioning?

66 The baptism of new Christians was truly fulfilled as they in turn began to share the gospel with others, hence keeping the missionary cycle going. 99
A. THEODORE EASTMAN

- **Working for a good end:** given new life through Christ's death and Resurrection, we are also called to be a sign of God's final purposes for creation. Personally we are on pilgrimage, working towards what God would have us be. As members of the church community, we are to relate together in such a way as to show God's life at work and to be co-workers in the locality. In our separate opportunities we show our discipleship by co-operating in the places where we meet others each day, to bring Resurrection life to all. Reflect on how this is brought out in the Communion service when we proclaim our faith in the Christ who has died, is risen and will come again. How can our church, in all the different gifts and ministries of all its members, be a sign of 'God's Kingdom come on earth as in Heaven'?

66 living in ... communion with God, all members of the church are called to confess their faith and to give an account of their hope. They are to identify with the joys and sufferings of all peoples as they seek to witness in caring love. The members of Christ's body are to struggle with the oppressed towards that freedom and dignity promised with the coming of the Kingdom. This mission needs to be carried out in varying political, social and cultural contexts. 99
WCC, LIMA: BAPTISM, EUCHARIST, MINISTRY

Co-operating with God's work in the world

We have one faith, but four Gospels. The New Testament reveals how churches in different places presented the gospel in ways suitable to the local people.

Compare (by reading some verses aloud) the gospel to the Jews (e.g. Acts 2.14–47, 3.11–26, 7.1–53; 13.16–41) and to the Greeks (e.g. Acts 10.34–43; 14.8–18, 17.22–34).

Discover what was the good news in those days for women, for men, for children, for slaves – see Jesus' attitudes and Paul's further challenges.

No church, alone, can expect to work equally and always at all Five Marks of Mission (how many can you name? See page ix!). The location in which your church is placed will determine your priorities – just as the gospel you proclaim will have a transforming influence on your neighbourhood.

> 66 The Gospel of Jesus Christ is ultimately concerned with the messianic preparation of our world to become the kingdom of God. 99
> EDWARD SCHILLEBEECKX

Many different forms of ministry

If you are a baptized Christian you are by definition a minister – whether you choose to acknowledge it or not. In this church of which the New Testament used the word *Koinonia* (communion) no one can actually be superior or inferior to another because all share equally in the ministry of Jesus and the life of the Holy Spirit. All of us together are invited to grow into the priesthood of the baptized, as we work for the coming of the Kingdom.

1 COR. 12–14; JOHN 4, 16.12–15; ACTS 1.8; EPH. 1.3–10; REV. 7.15–17

Local Ministry is not a fashionable stop-gap because of clergy shortages, although even if we wanted to we can no longer plan to staff the parishes in the ways to which we have been accustomed.

The Church of England's Advisory Board of Ministry (now Ministry Division of the Archbishop's Council) in its 1998 Annual Report announced a third year in which there was a significant rise in the number of candidates recommended for ordained ministries in all categories – the fifth in a rising trend. It is clear however that the numbers of retirements and the fact that many newly ordained are in mid-life mean that the ratio of stipendiary clergy to parishes continues to decline. The ministry of Readers is being systematically integrated into the overall structures. Normally any Reader in a parish would be expected to take a full part in a Ministry Leadership Team. This raises questions about selection and training (initial and continuing). Ordained Local Ministry becomes an increasingly significant factor in the life of

> 66 To become a genuinely missionary church we must engage in struggle alongside those in distress. 99
> ANN MORISY

ministry teams and parishes. We shall return to this topic in Stage Six.

Vocations to non-stipendiary ordained ministry are increasing at the present time, as many such clergy earn their living principally in secular employment, and so unless someone is retired, availability to the local church is usually limited.

The challenge is to see how a true partnership of many ministries can replace the inherited pattern in which there was a collusion of immature dependence between clergy and laity.

Experience shows that as churches move away from hierarchical ways of being governed towards partnerships echoing God's own trinitarian life, there is confusion and pain as well as delight.

In many parishes laity 'help' clergy who have 'delegated' some of their work to those who are willing. Some laity describe this as freeing the vicar for his or her real and important task. Important as this stage has been, 'helping the vicar' is not partnership ministry because it does not fully recognize the proper baptismal gifts and responsibilities of all.

66 From the very beginning of our commitment, directly if it be an adult or indirectly if it be an infant, there is a community which receives us, for it is together that we are meant to live the mystery of God taking possession of humanity. 99
LEON-JOSEPH SUENENS

1 COR. 12.4–31 ESP. VV. 8–11 AND 28

Together in mission and ministry

Who is God calling – here and now?

Read the following passages often used for Christian initiation:

- Matthew 28.16–20

- Romans 6.3–4

- 1 Corinthians 12–13

- 1 Peter 2.4–5.

Write up on a large sheet of paper the group's understanding of the connection between baptism and confirmation and your own ministries.

With the whole of your church in mind, reflect on the idea that baptism calls everyone repeatedly to conversion of life and calls us to take our share in Christ's own mission and ministry both in the church and the world.

66 key New Testament description of Jesus' ministry, and therefore of the church's leaders, is 'servant' meaning literally to be at the disposal of those at table and fulfilling their needs. 99
MARK 9.35

Read the following passages which open up the breadth of God's call:

- Romans 12.2–18
- Ephesians 4.11–16
- Matthew 28.16–20
- Mark 1.14–20
- Ezekiel 36.25a, 26–28.

Summarize on paper any further thoughts from this discussion to be fed into the overall process of discussions in your church.

Take time to recall and think about the images for church and ministry which the Bible offers.

Note how many images stress interdependence, rather than isolation.

Called to grow in Christ

In pairs read John 15.1–11. What is God saying to you about your ministry today?

Jeremiah 17.7–8 uses the image of a tree. Reflect on the ministry of all the baptized – including yourselves – as a tree that is healthy and strong. As a tree needs deep roots to sustain all the branches, what deep roots are needed for partnership ministry in your church?

Finally, two questions for the group as a whole:

1 What are the most urgent calls to ministry that we are experiencing in our lives?

2 Are the roots in place to sustain these different ministries?

Receiving reports from each group meeting in your local church will give a wide picture of the various types of ministry to which members are called – invite a group to make a display to show the congregation how together you express in your life and work your character as God's people.

Foretaste of God's reign

To let you sum up your hope for the 'holistic' development of your church's life and work, draw a poster of the

66 Baptism is ordination to the principal order of ministry. The first ministers of the church were all lay persons. Distinctions between Christians initially seem to have been made on the basis of individual gifts or specific functions, not on the basis of hierarchical office. 99
A. THEODORE EASTMAN

66 The tree is my eternal salvation. It is my nourishment and my banquet ... as it sighs around me in the breeze I am nourished with delight ... set firm between heaven and earth, base of everything that exists. 99
ST JOHN CHRYSOSTOM

66 There is no holiness but social holiness. 99
JOHN WESLEY

church as a signpost pointing to what God has in mind for the whole of creation *in your local setting.*

Warning!

So often our church agendas get reduced to a survival strategy of 'parish pump' ministry. Check you are keeping a proper balance between the internal and external life of the church gathered and dispersed in all its members. The following exercise assures we need to be looking in four directions to know God's purposes for us.

- For your poster take a large sheet of paper. (See Figure 4.) It helps to use different coloured pens to distinguish the various parts of the figure.

- Write in large letters, as background to the whole space, 'God's whole work in the world'.

- Write in the centre 'our local church now' – of course your church is not the hub of a wheel, but you are specifically asking what is your role here, in relation to everything else and in the wider context.

- Draw four arrow lines out from the centre.

- Label the end of each arrow respectively: **Jesus**, **Worshipping community**, **Context** and **God's kingdom**. It is impossible to separate out where God's spirit is active, but experience of using this model suggests that these four headings offer a vital way into discussing the whole picture. This exercise should be seen in relation to *Practising Community* (Robin Greenwood) pages 57–59.

66 We are called to be partners with God in his continuing work of creation within the personal, corporate and global spheres of life. We are called to be partners with Christ as he frees and empowers individuals, institutions and nations to fulfil their God-given possibilities. We are called to be partners with the spirit as she works for justice, peace and the unity of human kind. We are called to be patterns with all those who work to further human dignity within the bounds of our common humanity. 99
DAVID CLARK

66 Read ... like a Tracker: with your eyes on the ground and the horizon simultaneously. 99
HANNAH NYALA

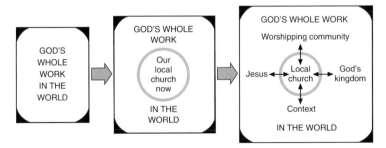

Figure 4

23

❝ If our religion is fundamentally irrelevant to our politics, then we are recognizing the political as a realm outside the reign of God. To divide the sacred from the secular is to recognize God's action only with the narrowest limits. **❞**
ALASTAIR MACINTYRE

❝ Yes, we are called to be bearers of tradition ... from Miriam to Isaiah to Jesus, from Hilda of Whitby to Hildegarde of Bingen, from Francis of Assisi to Dorothy Day and Petra Kelly, from Felicitas and Perpetua of North Africa to Archbishop Romero of El Salvador, these prophets of authentic ecclesia are the memory which liberates us and they go on before us calling us to build communities of integrity, 'until the dawn comes and the morning star rises in your minds'. **❞**
MARY C. GREY

Discuss together and write up:

- exactly how you see links between different moments of the Christian past (especially the work of Jesus Christ) and this moment;
- how the Holy Spirit through worship, study and fellowship is constantly showing new truths (John 16.13);
- what urgent needs and opportunities in your context do you need to address now, and what skills and wisdom can you bring to bear from secular life?
- how are you a sign and foretaste of God's reign in this place?

Is there a short slogan that comes out of the process, to put up over the poster?

Summarize the key points on which you want to focus:

- What does Jesus and 2,000 years of tradition so far tell you about the nature and quality of your ministry here and now?
- What is the Spirit showing you now about your next steps in mission and ministry?
- Specifically, how can you work with God in your locality?
- Which parts of the Kingdom agenda will you take on now?
- Remembering that we live by grace, how will you place proper limits on your hopes and plans? How will you prioritize?
- What strategies and materials will you need to put in place courses which allow the whole of your church to discover their gifts and ministries? Begin to make suggestions or get a group to research this.

What Leadership Do
You Need?

Stage One was about the present – in your neighbourhood and local church. Stage Two offered the stuff of which dreams are made – what is God calling your Christian community to be and do and with whom? An invitation to explore, get excited and take risks. Now we begin to ask, practically speaking, how shall we develop our vision? What forms of leadership will assist in bringing it about?

66 Of course, it is not just the Church that is talking about co-operating to get things done. Co-operation and teamwork are on every manager's agenda. 99
DERRICK ROWLAND

What Leadership?

All human endeavour requires leaders and leadership, yet history shows that solo-flight leaders with strong vision

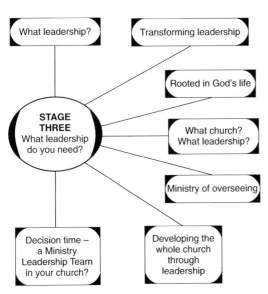

Figure 5 What leadership does your church now require?

66 In *Beyond the Dark Night: A Way Forward for the Church* Mary Grey promotes leaderships for church and society which are empowering and authorizing, rather than dominating and authoritarian, and spiritualities which are communal, mystical and not exclusive to church membership. 99
BERNARD KILROY

66 The call to the theological formation of the laos is more than call to teaching new skills and educational programs under the old paradigm, it is not simply providing lay training on the many 'how to's'; it is not simply a call to a new responsibility. Much deeper and more radical, it is a call to a new sensibility, to a new way of thinking, dwelling, deciding and acting. In short, it is a call to a new paradigm. 99
ELEAZAR S. FERNANDEZ

can sometimes be a disaster. Even now as we contemplate collaborative ministry in the church, there are plenty of strands of energy around, including in ourselves, that long for dependency on strong figures who in turn will get the blame when things go wrong. 'Vicar, tell us what to believe' meets with the response, 'Rosemary, if I told you, you wouldn't believe me.' In the group, share your own worst memories of leadership and contrast these with examples of good leaders you have known. How far are group members able to share reflection on their own practice of leadership in various situations?

The kind of organization we have in our churches – how people are regarded, led, managed and governed – is very important because it makes a vital practical statement about our 'Good News'.

In Stage One you looked at examples of instability and change in the world today. Old assumptions about where people stand towards one another are shifting rapidly – teachers and pupils, police with public, monarch with subjects, managers with employees and so on. Despite continued preoccupation with individual success and fulfilment, increasingly there are moves to develop corporate identity which includes diversity.

Create a collage picture together from newspapers which builds a visual image of the tensions inherent in modern society and shows what different leadership styles people adopt. Display your finished collage and use it to pray for world leaders and also those who feel disempowered.

Transforming Leadership

There is much talk these days about 'chaos theory'. The world may be better characterized as normally unstable with occasional signs of reliability, rather than assuming the opposite. Inherited certainties are no longer available to us. Do we lament this or learn to play in the space between order and disorder? How much order and governance does God want for his church, balanced by how much spontaneity, charisma, risk-taking and seizing of opportunity?

Chaos theory talks about:

1 The random connection between the flapping of a butterfly's wings in the Andes and a hurricane thousands of miles away. The point is that a tiny difference can lead to enormous unpredictable consequences.

2 Global order that on closer inspection is not usually peaceful and occasionally disordered, but the opposite, usually random with occasional stability: stochastic randomness is a complex form of order, allowing necessary change for survival in new circumstances.

3 Self-motivated organization, rather than enforced from outside or from above, as the true key to innovation, creativity and regeneration (Greek: *autopoesis* = self-ordering).

What is Teamwork?

Working as a team enable us to:

• do multi-faceted jobs by bringing together different skills;

• bring the resources of several minds to bear on problems and situations;

• achieve more in a sustainable form;

• provide support for otherwise isolated individuals.

So instead of fighting for more control from the centre or more freedom from the edge in an organization, why don't we work at interdependence – so everyone wins and no one loses and everyone owns the result?

To do this the church needs leaders who are capable of creating these conditions through:

1 **Judgement** – able to empower people to use their own judgement, and recognize shifting patterns. So the one in charge encourages others to be intuitive as well as to have the discernment to know which parts of the past tradition to rework.

2 **Coherence** – everyone knows the stated aims and objectives of their organization. For short periods there are focus groups on key issues.

3 **Review** – review is continuous, changing practice.

66 Elizabeth Johnson invites Christian communities to reinvent themselves in complex response to the Greek language of the Trinity – Perichoresis – which means a revolving action. 'We can say that the eternal flow of life is stepped to the contagious rhythms of spicy salsas, meringues, calypsos or reggaes where dancers in free motion are yet bonded to the music – the exuberant movement of equal relations.' 99
ELIZABETH JOHNSON

66 One thing institutions fear more than anything else is disorder, and you cannot change without the cards being reshuffled as it were. 99
HANNAH WARD AND JENNIFER WILD

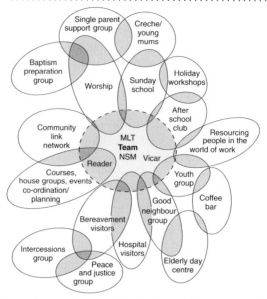

- The Team is there to support, encourage, link, reflect, generate ideas, serve, care, love, discern.
- The Team works with/under the guidance of the church council – together prioritizing and checking out direction.
- The Team is the servant of the ministry of the people – never a management elite.

Figure 6 A model for a developing ministry – some or all of these activities – and more besides.

66 God's promise to God's people – a relationship of covenant – decisively shapes how that community is then to live in righteousness with itself and others. 99
ELAINE GRAHAM

66 Christianity, for the first time in its history, is faced with a large-scale challenge to the patriarchal interpretation of religion and an increasingly coherent vision of an alternative way of constructing the tradition from its roots. 99
ROSEMARY RADFORD RUETHER

There is no blame, no scapegoating. Forgiveness and the recognition that everyone is involved in everything are key characteristics.

Discuss in the group how church leadership often gets distorted.

Looking at the following short statements, tell stories about real people you have known and your reaction to them. Beware of the need for confidentiality:

- Leadership has been too centred in the clergy.

- Our picture of Jesus has been coloured too much by the idea of kingship or ruler, justifying top-down hierarchy.

- We have forgotten that Jesus recognized that the poor and vulnerable have a significant and mysterious part in God's plans.

- Leadership becomes merely formal and seems not to be infused with God's presence.

Rooted in God's Life

A church that echoes God's trinitarian life will be working towards modelling partnerships of many kinds – young and old, rich and poor, people of differing educational training, laity and ordained – accepting all, in their difference, having vitality and equal value.

Baptism is the key to all ministry – so not even Archbishops or Archdeacons can in the order of God's Kingdom in fact be superior to or of more value than the tiniest babe in arms.

In a church ordered by a trinitarian God, inequality is not on. We see this in the attitude fostered by Jesus among his closest followers: it was hard enough for them while he was with them – no wonder we still struggle.

Eastern theology uses the word *perichoresis* to speak of God as difference in unity – where there is all the richness of diversity and complexity (see Robin Greenwood, *Transforming Priesthood. A New Theology of Mission and Ministry*, pp 82–83, 116, 156).

Church members are often in the front line of encouraging peaceful diversity, e.g. in multifaith neighbourhoods, in the complexity of a school staffroom, or in local politics. In Stage Two you looked at key theological ideas – church as community (*koinonia*), as finding identity in partnership, echoing trinitarian life, as sign of the coming reign of God, as always mutual partnership. What will this mean now as you are asking questions about leadership?

How are your church's ministries modelled on the ministry of Jesus?

- Choosing to take up the cross and dying daily in costly choices?

- Not being afraid to stand with the least important?

- Unmasking status and removing barriers of race, religion, class, gender?

- Speaking and acting authentically out of a passionate vision of what God wants for the wholeness of all creation?

66 praise, gratitude, joy and enjoyment. 99
PS. 145

66 'God is' is the supreme prophetic statement, the discernment which can illuminate all discernment and action. But it is not a statement about something static and fixed: it is about a God who is alive, active, listening and communicating. To recognise this God in each situation is always the most urgent priority. 99
DANIEL W. HARDY AND DAVID F. FORD

LUKE 12.49–56

66 It must become clear that church members who deny in fact their responsibility for the needy in any part of the world are just as guilty of heresy as those who deny this or that article of faith. 99
VISSER'T HOOFT

- Not offering glib answers but helping others make connections for themselves through feelings, bodies and minds?

- Working persuasively, humbly and gently in mutual regard (Matthew 11.12)?

Do you find yourselves expecting the blessings of God and the gifts of the Holy Spirit?
Are you:

- Promoting partnership rather than individualistic faith and action among disciples?

- Working with partner churches unless some very good reason prevents for a time (find out more about the witness of the Iona Community in which every act of worship is ecumenical)? There is only one mission for one world – the mission of the triune God in which we share in all our diversity.

- Subverting the world's culture of overwork, by negotiating with all leaders not only role- but time-commitment?

- In a relationship of radical dependence on God's grace (Matt. 5.1–12)?

- Being a church where everyone in their need – material and spiritual – can expect abundance?

- Expecting to know Jesus Christ in serving the needs of the 'least' of our sisters and brothers (Matt. 10.4–42)?

- Remaining hopeful and courageous in the face of failure and opposition?

- Willing to oppose systems and people that bring injustice?

- Puropsefully expecting transformation in world and church, working with imagination for the coming of God's Kingdom of which our church is a sign?

What Can We Learn From the Scriptures?
From the earliest days of the church different emphases have been placed on such images as:

Pilgrim People

> 66 Yesterday I saw a stranger,
> I put meat in the eating place,
> Water in the drinking place,
> Music in the listening place.
> And the lark said in her song –
> 'often, often goes the Christ in the stranger's guise'. 99

GAELIC RUNE OF HOSPITALITY
QUOTED BY DOUGLAS GALBRAITH

Body of Christ

Light of the World

Bride of Christ

Sacrament of God's presence

Rock

Salt

Ark of Salvation

Other

On your own first, decide which two of these carry most meaning for you – think of real examples in church life of the examples you've chosen. Now share this in the group and note the range of views.

In a similar way differing images of leadership and ministry have abounded. Our vision grows small when we over-emphasize just one or two of them and forget the rest. The existence of a variety of leadership gifts corresponds to the fact that there are a variety of leadership functions necessary within the church. It is therefore not surprising that the evidence of the New Testament suggests that from the beginning a corporate leadership was the norm. Nowhere do we discern anyone who might be described in modern terms as 'the minister' of a local church.

Looking up the following passages and many more for yourselves will serve to illustrate the enormous variety of different titles and experiments in ministry within the early church. Attach to each one examples of your own life experience.

1 disciples sent by Jesus (Mark 1.16–20; Luke 24.44–49);

2 witnesses of the Resurrection (1 Cor. 15.3–7; Acts 10.39–42);

3 preachers of the good news (Acts 2.14; 4.33–35);

4 leaders in prayer, teaching and service (Acts 2.42–47; 6.2–4);

5 judges of the new Israel (Matt. 19.28; Luke 22.28–30);

6 local ministers (Acts 13.1–3; Rom. 12.6ff – no clear pattern);

❝ The ministry of the Church is a corporate one in the church's task, but the ordained minister recognizing the activity of God in and for this corporate ministry, represents it to the members of the church, focuses and collects it in a co-ordinated pattern and distributes it in the service of God's work in the world.

But this work is achieved only in so far as the community of the church recognizes, trusts and sustains the ordained minister in the faith integrity, hope, love and vision and by which he or she recognizes the activity of God, in God, in it.

Corporate and ordained ministry, therefore, animate each other, each focusing the activity of God, the working of the Holy Spirit in the other. ❞
ACCM OCCASIONAL PAPER 22

7 administrator (1 Cor. 12.28);

8 one who takes the lead (1 Thess. 5.12; Rom. 12.8);

9 service (Mark 9.33–35; John 12.1–7);

10 many titles linked to the ministry of Jesus: servant, apostle, evangelist, prophet, teacher, shepherd, priest ...

You will have noted three obvious dangers in this process:

- working with only one or two metaphors and ignoring the rest;

- loading these ideas only into the ministry of the ordained;

- assuming that 'our' preferred or inherited pattern or vocabulary is somehow 'OK' or specially approved by God.

Different church communities in various contexts and historical moments have always found some words more helpful than others, perhaps reacting to counterbalance the overuse of some terms. Those in the group who have in their lifetime belonged to successive churches may be more aware of this than others.

Overseeing

Nothing in this handbook denies the value of ordained ministry – provided we are clear what it's for. There is a persistent danger that ordained persons are seen as a substitute for the proper ministry of others. The ordained are those uniquely called, not to some generalized notion of leadership, but to minister 'the one body and one spirit', the 'one hope of your calling' among those whose differing ministries may carry them in different directions. What does 'leadership' mean for being a vicar or assistant priest today and in the years ahead? Increasingly there are suggestions that the kind of overseeing role the Bishop aims to have in the diocese, the parish priest carries out for the local church.

Power is in the networks of entire community, never possessed by one and not by another. All the members need is help in knowing and taking their proper place – and no more than that. This makes fine theory for talking

George Mcleod, who prompted the rebuilding of the abbey on Iona, is famed for describing Iona as 'a thin place' where only a tissue separates us from the holy. Likewise, being alongside those who are poor and excluded can also be 'a thin place'. It can be 'Bethel', the place of God.
ANN MORISY

Fear among priests or lay people that collaboration will undermine priests or leave them with little to do. This may combine with a sense of loss of identity especially as competent and qualified lay people may be more successful in animating some aspects of pastoral life than priests.
THE SIGN WE GIVE (BISHOPS' CONFERENCE OF ENGLAND AND WALES)

of our church as the body of Christ, but in reality we all come with disabilities, fears and histories which contribute to the distortion of mutual relations. All the more reason for a corporate leadership that is aware of the power imbalances and which can contribute to healing and restoration.

Use the following quotatations – and ones from other sources to stimulate debate:

The role of the priest is to lift up and enrich others, who themselves are called to a variety of ministries. So the priest is not a substitute for others, displaying the ministries to which laity are called by baptism, but is to support them, drawing upon the same active spirit of Christ which enriches others in ministry. Priests are to recall other ministries to the marks of the Church, holiness, catholicity and apostolicity, above all through the worship of the church at which the priest presides.

Daniel W. Hardy

The fundamental role of the leader is to make collegiality possible. The role of the one in charge is not that of making a 'personal' decision. His(her) role is rather to make it possible in so far as it depends on him(her), for there to be a common decision which commits each member to the decision. A true leader will find his(her) place when (s)he has succeeded in helping others to find theirs.

Leon-Joseph Suenens

The ordained minister needs to be one chosen because he or she has the gifts, resources and wisdom constantly to represent the mind of Christ in the church, as it were holding up a mirror to the congregation and asking 'are we a true community of Jesus Christ?'. So the chief service of the church leader is that of maintaining a Christian community true to the heart of Jesus and his message, in whatever circumstances and society, it finds itself.

Robin Greenwood

Also see the Web site for the 1999 International Symposium on Local/ Total/Common Ministry in San Francisco: http://totalministry.org.

Increasingly, clergy are learning to hold together both team membership and leadership. Many see themselves as having an 'oversight' ministry in a parish or wider area.

66 We will reflect together on the needs and challenges facing us … we will evaluate the resources we have and how best to use them … we will do our best to work collaboratively with each other so that the result is a real 'conspirio' – a breathing together of the breath of the Holy Spirit who inspires all our work and leads us ever more deeply into the truths of the Gospel. 99
CRISPIN HOLLIS

66 Perhaps the church's main contribution is to be a good learning community itself, where there is joy in knowledge, understanding, insight and wisdom. Can it be a place where people learn to love God with all their minds and to relate everything – all fields of knowledge and all of life – to who God is and what God does? 99
DAVID F. FORD

66 I do not believe that we will recover the sense of being the body of Christ in our time until there is a revolution in our practice of baptism comparable to that which has occurred in the eucharistic celebration.

The early Christian movement saw itself as the body of Christ, created in the act of baptism and constantly renewed in the eucharistic offering. Throughout the Pauline letters the church is called 'the body of Christ' (1 Cor. 12.27; Eph.1.23). It is this sense of being in the body of Christ the organism of the crucified and risen Christ, which constitutes the primary liturgical consciousness. The community seeks the fullness of Christ in the building up of the body (Eph. 4.13). 99

KENNETH LEECH

In the group, reflect together on the qualities and tasks required in clergy when the whole church is recognized as a body of ministers part of 'the priesthood of all believers'. Explore the role of the parish priest.

1 In terms of a ministry of **presiding** unpacked with the three ideas of **discerning**, **blessing** and **witnessing**.

2 As an instrument of the marks of the church in the creed – one called to build up the church in **oneness**, **holiness**, **catholicity** and **apostolicity** especially through the preaching of the Word and the celebration of worship.

Be specific about what is the practical outworking of these gifts and tasks for the building up of your church. Who else exercises parallel gifts in the neighbourhood?

Figure 7, illustrates in caricature form three models of ministry which we find in churches today.

Model One – the collusion that the clergy (with Readers) are to provide professional services for people, such as leading worship, visiting, preaching, and so on.

Model Two – because the vicar is ill or has too much to do, others – by delegation – are sometimes 'allowed to help' him/her in carefully supervised ways.

Model Three – all Christians by baptism share Christ's ministry for the world. This is a church *of* not just *for* people. The priest is actually called to be minister of unity, allowing for the mutuality of difference in relation. The priest 'holds the ring' (presides/oversees) in that (s)he invokes in all ministries that which gives

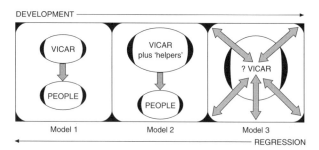

Figure 7 Three models of ministry.

the church its specific missionary character – holiness, catholicity and apostolicity.

Consider together:

1 In choosing to move away from Model One, what might be the advantages and problems?

2 If you are at Model One, would it help or hinder to skip over Model Two and go straight to Model Three?

3 Alternatively, do you want to keep bits of all three models working together?

4 Can you see times when Model One would be your preference? Are there particular ministries which belong only to the clergy?

There is plenty of evidence in the Church of England, and in other churches, that paternalism, hierarchy and discipline are preferred and that open forms of leadership are feared and disliked. We need to be aware of our own personal histories and cultural memories which colour our own preferences about status and formality.

Discuss in the group how you would want to see partnership developing in the following areas:

- worship
- witnessing in the workplace
- preaching
- evangelism
- the neighbourhood and global issues
- healing
- spiritual guidance
- administration
- preparation for sacraments
- pastoral visiting
- community projects.

Ask yourselves how you see partnership in these spheres. What is there that you believe only the clergy should be doing?

Ensure that each area of ministry has a person, small group or team responsible for it. How do each of these

66 Today spirituality is ecclesial and incarnational: it challenges us to serve the world and to become involved in social justice issues. We are no longer dealing with unusual ascetic practices but are concentrating on the basic life style implied in the universal baptismal vocation.

Each baptised person is called to the fullness of Christian life. 99
LEONARD DOOHAN

66 The nature of the church should manifest the nature of God. We are all members of a church on the way towards the full realization of God's life. 99
CATHERINE MOWRY LACUGNA

66 Every local Christian community contains within its membership all the resources necessary to function as a worshipping body. 99
ROLAND ALLEN

find support for and show accountability to the church council? How could this be further developed? Is there regular ministry in your church that is not supported, trained nor accountable? How can members of the public gain access to these ministries without having to go through the clergy all the time?

What real commitment and support are clergy and readers in your church willing to give to local ministry?

A Ministry Leadership Team For Your Church?

So, having come through this long process of discussion, now is the time to consider what kind of leadership you

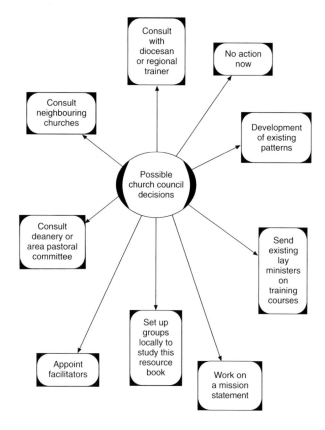

Figure 8 What next step should you take?

36

will need for the way you feel God is calling you in mission and ministry. What resources is God offering you from all the people in your church? We suggest you refer back now to the early descriptions of a Ministry Leadership Team in this resource book (especially pp. xvii–xxiii). Talk and pray your way to a consensus – you may need a day set aside or a residential weekend.

List and discuss the questions that arise for you that will need further clarification.

Figure 8 summarizes directions you might want to explore next. Stage Four offers figures to prompt your thinking. The key is to make decisions that will most helpfully serve your church in your situation now.

Keep in touch with the diocese or region about local ministry through the usual networks as well as special meetings, literature or conferences. Ensure members of your church read some of the books listed at the end of this handbook.

66 Jesus gave embodiment to the vulnerability of God, a God who shares the fragility and ambiguity of life on earth. There is no particular glory in being powerless. What we try to do is to crack open the myth on which public life is built, the defences built by the rich and powerful to avoid fear of death, sickness and mortality ... 99

MARY GREY

37

STAGE FOUR

Establishing a Local Ministry Leadership Team

One church council writes:

Local Ministry means for us: catching a vision and building up our confidence together as lay and ordained, so that the gifts we all have can be released and used – in ministry with the church and its mission and life in the world around us.

Our Ministry Leadership Team is a leading and enabling team – not there to do everything on behalf of everyone else, but to enable and encourage people to realize that we are being church together.

Local Ministry Leadership Teams are being established in a great variety of ways to carry forward a shared vision of where God is calling a parish church in a locality. Figure 9 shows how a MLT could provide a distributing focus to the work of many ministry teams in a complex urban, suburban, market town, or village location. There are endless possibilities, including the situation where every member of a small church would simply be the team. Obviously, every parish/benefice or cluster of local churches will make their own choices, but the following guidelines flow from current experience throughout the Anglican Communion.

It needs to be a priority that:

- you have long and careful discussion, preparation and shared vision setting, facilitated by those with appropriate experience, and so set clear terms of reference for the team;

- this process takes plenty of time and involves as many people as possible;

- team members are either chosen by the local people for a clearly defined task – or chosen for their gifts; and before specific tasks are discerned they need the

❝ To be Church today and to be relevant to the world in which we live we must tap and develop the rich variety of people's gifts from the Spirit. Just as parents must tap and develop the potentials of their children, so too all in the Church are called to discover and parent the unique individuality of each of the baptized. In building Christ's family, every baptized person has a part to play.

Christ continually distributes in His body, that is, in the Church, gifts of ministries in which, by His own power we serve each other unto salvation so that, carrying out the truth in love, we might through all things grow up into Him who is our head.

Nowadays we recognize that the development of family life is the responsibility of all members, and this is likewise the case for the Church. In ecclesial life this co-responsibility is required, not for efficiency or democracy but because of faith. Our faith in the Church needs to be expressed in all the members of this family working together. It is time for the courageous involvement of all people in the Church, together as one family. ❞
LEONARD DOOHAN

66 Clearly some form of
leadership is required but
ecclesial leadership is to be
rooted in the ministry of service,
not of lordship. Leadership within
the church must be submitted to
the power of the Spirit of God,
Spirit of Christ. Just as the divine
arche does not belong to one
person alone, the grace and
power of God are distributed
among all members of the
Church. Ministry is not the
'dispensing' of God's grace by the
elite to the many, but one of the
outward signs that the life of the
church is constituted by Christ
and the Spirit. Ministry properly
exercised activates the vocation
and mission of every member of
the Church to become
Christ. 99
CATHERINE MOWRY LACUGNA

support and affirmation of the church council/PCC and parish priest;

- team membership is monitored and renewed on a rolling programme (a term of three, four or five years); no member serves for more than three such terms;

- consideration is given to the overall age span of the MLT membership;

- the articulated and shared purpose is to move beyond laity just 'helping the Vicar' towards a genuine partnership of every ministry;

- a commitment to learning is an essential ingredient in the life of the team, and therefore of the whole church. This would include regular meetings with facilitators, specific skills training for individuals with members of other teams, and occasional joint residentials for several teams learning together from differing contexts.

Some will become members of a MLT automatically because of an existing role in the church, and others will be recommended because of the particular gifts/ skills a church is looking for to carry forward certain mission priorities.

It's vital that the entire local church take seriously its responsibility in choosing the members of a MLT:

- by shared thinking about these new roles of ministry for the congregation;

- by taking part in meetings and group study sessions;

- by daily prayer for discernment, reflecting on the leadership needs of a changing church;

- by considering specifically what God may ask of me;

- by being prepared to speak up with confidence either to support or question issues that affect the whole church.

Figure 9 highlights the key questions to be faced.

The Relationship Between a PCC and a MLT

Some parishes have been working for years on developing the role of their PCC in mission and ministry. In many

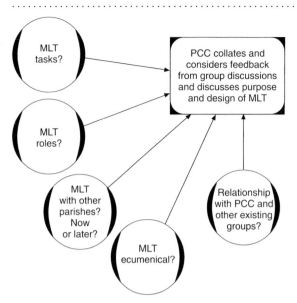

Figure 9 The relationship between a PCC and a MLT.

places we see church council sub-groups working on particular issues.

As you discuss the most appropriate developments for your church it will be vital to see a clear distinction between the specific tasks of the church council and a MLT, even if in the end you decide that one body can perform both tasks.

It may be helpful to refresh your understanding of the role of the PCC. In the Church of England the Parochial Church Council (Powers) Measure 1956, section 2, sees the PCC as holding responsibility with the parish priest for making sure the church fulfils its proper roles and functions.

In general, 'It shall be the duty of the minister (sic!) and the PCC to consult together on matters of general concern and importance to the parish.'

Some of the functions of the PCC are set out as: 'co-operation with the minister in promoting the mission of the church, pastoral, evangelistic, social and ecumenical'.

It's clear that a PCC is expected to realize that the Church of England is a community of communities in that its doctrine cannot be simplistically understood and

❝ Ministry as the sharing of God's gifts in service is the personal privilege and imperative of every member of the church by baptism. ❞
WESLEY FRENSDORFF

41

laid on members as an official line to be followed. Further, a PCC will be the point of contract between the particular parish and the wider church through deanery and diocese.

The PCC and the parish priest are clearly expected to be partners in all matters that do not involve the obvious confidentiality of one-to-one pastoral relationships.

There are very practical demands on a PCC about fabric and property maintenance, finance, the decisions connected with the Priests (Ordination of Women) Measure 1993, arrangements during a 'vacancy' (between one priest leaving and the arrival of another), the negotiations about a new priest's appointment, deciding on forms of church services, appointment of organists, negotiations about parishes joining together, formal co-operation between clusters of local clergy or church-sharing with other denominations.

The membership by law includes all licensed, serving clergy, deaconesses or lay workers licensed to the parish, churchwardens, and any person on the electoral roll who is a member of Deanery, Diocesan or General Synod. Readers may be members by local agreement or election. In addition there are elected and co-opted members as decided by the annual parochial meeting. More details will be found in chapter 3 of *Practical Church Management, A Guide for Every Parish*, by James Behrens.

The tenor of these expectations is apparently more about overall oversight of everything a parish might be concerned to be and do, rather than the specific task of a ministry team working to lead the development of the PCC's vision. However, that is for each local church to work out.

Ask yourself:

1 What are the key purposes of the PCC in the light of the legal framework?

2 How have you extended the basic expectations to meet your own particular needs and opportunities?

Together in the group draw a diagram that shows the role of your PCC as a whole in the parish, and the tasks of individual members or roles.

❝❝ Dear sisters and brothers, with the energy of the Holy Spirit let us tear apart all walls of civilization and the culture of death that separates us. And let us participate in the Holy Spirit's economy of life, fighting for our life on this earth in solidarity with all living beings and building communities for justice, peace and the integrity of creation. Wild wind of the Holy Spirit, blow to us. Let us welcome her, letting ourselves go to her wild rhythm of life. Come Holy Spirit, renew the whole creation. Amen! ❞❞

CHUNG HYUN KYUNG

With the introduction of a MLT thought needs to be given to its relationship with the PCC as confusion of roles could easily happen.

One possible distinction is to consider the PCC as having a 'diaconal' role (i.e. serving the church to make mission and ministry possible), while an 'apostolic' role is given to MLTs, readers and clergy.

To avoid muddling the two, consider the following:

- There is bound to be overlap in membership between a PCC and MLT.

- A PCC has the overall task with clergy of leading the whole life of the church.

- A PCC must ensure there is sufficient and appropriate ministry for the church's mission.

- A MLT provides a distributing focus for ministry.

- A MLT is an expansion of the clerical role of overseeing and leading the church's ministry.

- A MLT serves, nourishes and encourages the ministry *of all*.

- A MLT does not make parish policy; that is more properly the task of the PCC.

- A MLT is not just about the internal life of the church. Its membership should reflect the church's wide involvement in secular employment, local community and family life.

66 Power and authority can be exercised through domination, and they most frequently are, in a world patterned by patriarchal paradigms of reality. But they can also be exercised through empowerment and authorising, as they sometimes are where people are seeking to live out the gospel vision of shared community of service. 99
LETTY RUSSELL

You will have to make decisions about who will be members of the Ministry Leadership Team. Some will be there automatically because of an existing role in the church and others will be recommended because of the particular gifts/skill you are looking for to carry forward your mission priorities. You need to consult as widely as possible about choosing the membership. (See *Practising Community* by Robin Greenwood, chapter 1.)

A Model for Choosing the Team

Guidelines of the Diocese of Gloucester (adapted):

- General publicity about the idea of Local Ministry and the purpose of a MLT over a period of several months.

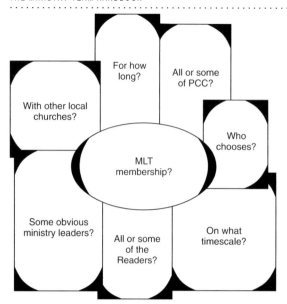

Figure 10 Key issues on the constitution of your Ministry Leadership Team.

> ❝ Is it possible to discern what the Holy Spirit is saying to the church? Perhaps we can only begin to do so in the conviction that others are listening too and that it is only in the to-and-fro of a shared dialogue that the whole truth can begin to emerge. ❞
>
> JOHN O'BRIEN CSSP

- A letter to all people on the electoral roll and as many other local people as possible, asking for suggestions for people with the skills and gifts needed for the Team.

- At a special PCC service the PCC makes recommendations about who to ask from the names suggested. Each PCC member is separately given a list of names and asked to make a confidential recommendation using this code:

  ☐ I recommend them strongly

  ☐ I recommend them

  ☐ I don't know them well enough to express an opinion

  ☐ I don't recommend that they are asked at the moment

- The vicar and facilitators (or diocesan officer) draw up a list of people to ask from the PCC recommendations in order to give a balanced team – of ages, of sexes, of gifts, of backgrounds, of availability.

Commissioning by the Bishop

The church and MLT need to mark rites of passage. The authorization negotiated with the Bishop or his representative makes the MLT more than a local or temporary initiative. It places it properly into the safe environment of the diocese whose role it is to nurtute and resource this development.

This Resource Book strongly recommends that you negotiate with your Bishop for recognition and commissioning of your MLT. The commissioning recommended here is not about individuals receiving titles and status. Rather it's a chance for your Bishop to hear and discuss your hopes and fears about partnership in ministry and publicly to affirm the fact that your parish now has a Ministry Leadership Team, whose membership and purpose has been carefully thought through and will be open to frequent review. Further, it will be treated by the Bishop as part of the normal provision of ministry.

Process for Commissioning

The Bishop (or representative) will have been involved at the point where the PCC decided to set up a MLT, and will have been kept informed of development.

After a period of two years, when it is clear that the MLT is working effectively and healthily, the PCC reviews its work and formally requests the Bishop's commission.

If the Bishop is satisfied that the MLT is exercising the ministry to which it is called in the context of its parish priest and PCC, he will in the course of public worship commission the parish a MLT – but not the individual members themselves. The creating of the worship for this occasion is a great opportunity for spelling out the entire vision not only in the text but in its public performance. The guest list needs to be carefully thought through also. Which other communities do you want to include in this key moment in the development of your local church?

Some of the benefits of having a commissioning service or statement from the Bishop would be:

- to help the process of defining your objectives;

- to challenge you to think of issues which otherwise might be overlooked;

❝ The Bible tells the story of the giant Goliath being defeated by little David. Another story tells of a little sparrow on its back in the road, its feeble legs flailing desperately in the air. A horseman comes riding by, reins in his horse and asks sarcastically 'what do you think you are doing?' 'Well', said the sparrow, 'I heard that the sky will fall in today and I am trying to hold it up.' The horseman said mockingly, 'And do you really think that you, feeble creature that you are, can make any difference to the scale of the disaster?' 'Well', said the sparrow, 'one does what one can.'❞

JOAN CHITTISTER (PARAPHRASED BY MARY GREY)

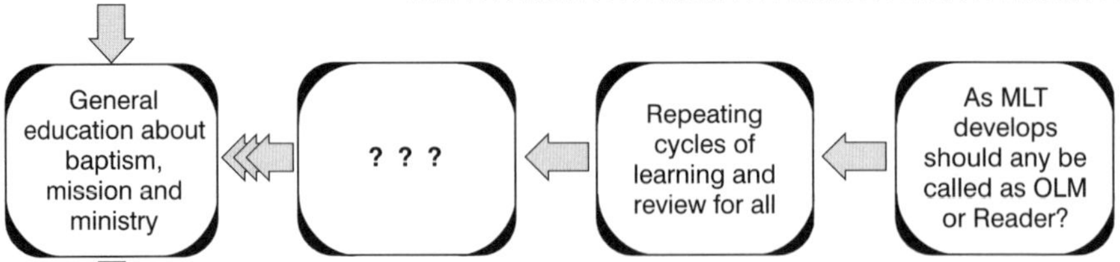

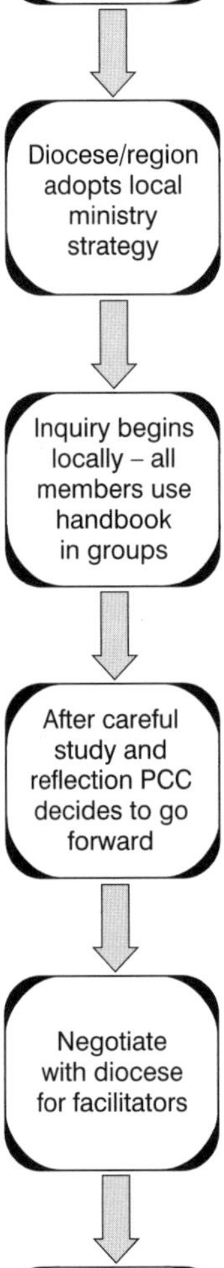

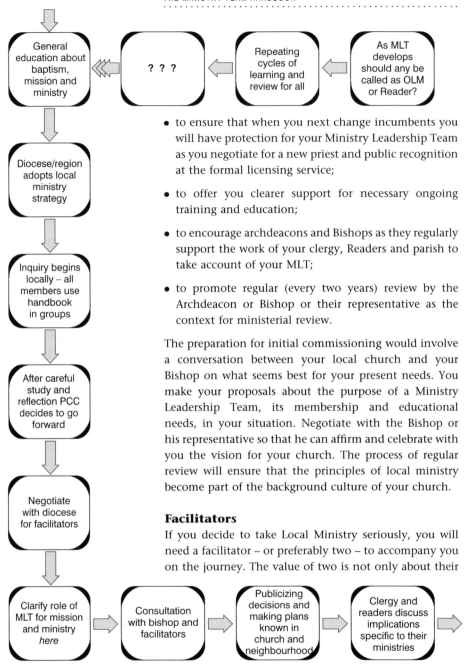

- to ensure that when you next change incumbents you will have protection for your Ministry Leadership Team as you negotiate for a new priest and public recognition at the formal licensing service;
- to offer you clearer support for necessary ongoing training and education;
- to encourage archdeacons and Bishops as they regularly support the work of your clergy, Readers and parish to take account of your MLT;
- to promote regular (every two years) review by the Archdeacon or Bishop or their representative as the context for ministerial review.

The preparation for initial commissioning would involve a conversation between your local church and your Bishop on what seems best for your present needs. You make your proposals about the purpose of a Ministry Leadership Team, its membership and educational needs, in your situation. Negotiate with the Bishop or his representative so that he can affirm and celebrate with you the vision for your church. The process of regular review will ensure that the principles of local ministry become part of the background culture of your church.

Facilitators

If you decide to take Local Ministry seriously, you will need a facilitator – or preferably two – to accompany you on the journey. The value of two is not only about their

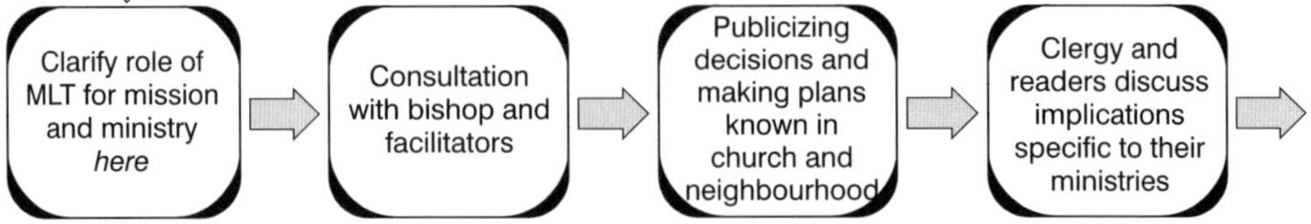

Figure 11 Flow chart for implementing a ministry leadership team.

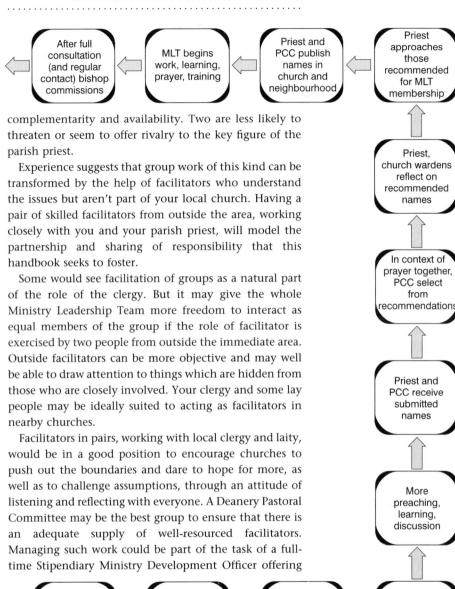

After full consultation (and regular contact) bishop commissions

MLT begins work, learning, prayer, training

Priest and PCC publish names in church and neighbourhood

Priest approaches those recommended for MLT membership

Priest, church wardens reflect on recommended names

In context of prayer together, PCC select from recommendations

Priest and PCC receive submitted names

More preaching, learning, discussion

complementarity and availability. Two are less likely to threaten or seem to offer rivalry to the key figure of the parish priest.

Experience suggests that group work of this kind can be transformed by the help of facilitators who understand the issues but aren't part of your local church. Having a pair of skilled facilitators from outside the area, working closely with you and your parish priest, will model the partnership and sharing of responsibility that this handbook seeks to foster.

Some would see facilitation of groups as a natural part of the role of the clergy. But it may give the whole Ministry Leadership Team more freedom to interact as equal members of the group if the role of facilitator is exercised by two people from outside the immediate area. Outside facilitators can be more objective and may well be able to draw attention to things which are hidden from those who are closely involved. Your clergy and some lay people may be ideally suited to acting as facilitators in nearby churches.

Facilitators in pairs, working with local clergy and laity, would be in a good position to encourage churches to push out the boundaries and dare to hope for more, as well as to challenge assumptions, through an attitude of listening and reflecting with everyone. A Deanery Pastoral Committee may be the best group to ensure that there is an adequate supply of well-resourced facilitators. Managing such work could be part of the task of a full-time Stipendiary Ministry Development Officer offering

Preaching, learning, discussing how MLT will affect everyone

In the light of your mission aims, what tasks, roles, skills in MLT?

PCC discusses and communicates to *all* the next stages

Written suggestions for MLT limited

47

education and training for ministry across one or several deaneries or clusters of churches.

In particular facilitators can:

- help people to express and deal with their own and others' feelings;
- help with the expression, exploration and possible resolution of conflict;
- help create an environment of acceptance of difference;
- value the individuals, the group and the task – encourage the balancing of all three;
- ensure that everyone is heard.

As need arises, the diocese will build up a network of facilitators who will be vigorously selected for their potential in this particularly demanding but rewarding ministry. Hopefully, people who have relevant experience and qualifications from other parts of their lives will offer themselves for this work. After a short induction, there needs to be regular training and support to help facilitators reflect on their work, and periodic review of their progress and effectiveness.

> ❝We did not want it easy, God,
> But we did not contemplate
> That it would be quite this hard,
> This long, this lonely.
> So, if we are to be turned inside out,
> And upside down,
> With even our pockets shaken
> Just to check what's rattling
> And left behind,
> We pray that you will keep faith with us,
> And we with you,
> Holding our hands as we weep,
> Giving us strength to continue,
> And showing us beacons
> Along the way
> To becoming new. ❞
>
> ANNA MCKENZIE IN SHEILA CASSIDY

Facilitator Profile
Education and qualifications
Probably educated beyond secondary school level. Has continued with education throughout adult life so far.

Experience and training
Experience of and commitment to collaborative ways of working.
Has worked with groups as manager, facilitator, trainer, consultant or experimental educator/trainer.
Has worked in voluntary organizations.
Interested and aware of group processes.
Aware of and has learnt from own experiences of working in groups.
Ideally has had some training in group process and/or management tasks and people.

Personal qualities
Articulate
Reflective
Sensitive
Flexible
Perceptive
Courageous

Mental and emotional attributes
Eager to explore and understand the dynamics of a working group.
Willing to accept difference.
Able to tolerate and explore causes of conflict.
Aware of boundaries – personal, psychological – and their role.

A facilitator of Local Ministry writes
It has been a joy to go back and visit one of these worshipping communities, to revisit their mission statement. I found a transformed worshipping community. There was an air of gentle confidence around. New ministries had been raised up in the areas of funerals, service leading, preaching, children's liturgy, pastoral visiting, administration and others. Two areas in the parish had raised up priests and a deacon had just been ordained. Here was a community alive to the needs and challenges of ministry and mission. There were still problems to be addressed and gaps in training and resources to be filled but they had walked through death and been resurrected to new life. No one said it would be easy!

The need for regional support
Experience in different regions and dioceses varies considerably. There can be no blueprint about facilitators – only the will to experiment and monitor what works and what fails. Essentially what is required is for those charged with overseeing and developing the church at a regional level to be proactive and imaginative in finding the best support for supporting new patterns of ministry locally.

Implications for Ordained Ministers
Most clergy have been formed in a rather individualistic model of ministry and need support in developing

❝ No ministry in the Church can be understood outside the context of the community. This should not be explained in terms of representativeness and delegation of authority, for these terms being basically juridical finally lead to a separation of the ordained person from the community: to act *on behalf* of the community means to stand *outside* it because it means to act *in its place*. But what is precisely denied by this communal dimension is that there is no ministry then can stand *outside* or *above* the community. ❞
JOHN D. ZIZIOULAS

Sometimes tradition seems frozen under a great ice shell but below this frozen and rigid surface flow ever fresh springtime waters. It is up to us, with the help of God's grace, to break the ice that is above all the ice of our hearts become cold ... From the ancient spring we will drink water that will give us a new force so as to answer the questions of today.

ELIZABETH BEHR-SIGEL 🙶

relationships of accountability. It is made harder because church communities have more often been a collection of ministry individuals rather than a ministry collective, and it can be a struggle for everyone. Churches exploring Local Ministry will need to spend time thinking about the implications of this for ordained clergy and especially for parish priests. There will be additional issues if in a cluster of several local churches there is just one vicar. The inherited tradition of most churches is of clergy displacing the proper ministry of the laity because that was the expectation. Local ministry accelerates the current move towards clergy who are selected, trained and self-aware as trainers, enablers, teachers, leaders, overseers and those who represent the local church to other churches and communities. As a Bishop is to a diocese so is a priest to the local church. These issues are explored in detail in both *Transforming Priesthood* and *Practising Community* by Robin Greenwood. Lay involvement makes more demands on clergy.

In your group of clergy and lay together, make a list of ten characteristics of clergy as the church needs them now and in the future, expanding the clues offered below:

1 appropriate responsibility

2 resourcing others

3 team workers

4 presiding

5 shared not delegated ministry

6 vulnerable

7 agents of change

8 pastors

9 making connections

10 links with society.

Local Ministry is not a superficial matter of rearranging tasks and roles. The hearts and minds of every member of the church will need to be changed for true partnership in ministry to have a chance to develop.

Keeping a Ministry Leadership Team Healthy

Churches often suffer short-term initiative fatigue. Developing Local Ministry for mission is a long-term goal which if it is to persist needs strategies for sustenance, feeding and replenishing. This is more than pulling out the stops to 'survive' a vacancy between vicars, and more than helping the clergy. The role of diocese or region for local churches now is to provide an environment in which a partnership vision for mission and ministry is seen as just normal and ordinary and is lightly but surely resourced. So what precisely is needed for sustainability – both in the local church and from outside?

> 66 People who trust in God know that God is waiting for them, that they are invited to God's future, so that they are holding in their hands the most marvellous invitation they have ever had in their lives. 99
> JÜRGEN MOLTMANN

Reflecting, Developing, Connecting, Revisioning

In a healthy team:

- Self-directional learning, reflection, prayer and mutual support will take place, resourced by facilitators from outside the parish.

- Meetings will need to be planned in diaries well in advance and then defended.

- Members will find ways of gaining a sense of having equal significance, despite their differing personalities and roles.

- Confidentiality both about work undertaken among people and within the MLT meeting itself needs to be strictly agreed.

> 66 There is no light without shadow, and no wholeness without imperfection. To round itself out, life calls not for perfection but for completeness. 99
> C. G. JUNG

Getting started – allowing for different feelings and energy levels

In any team, members will arrive with:

- a strong sense of commitment and achievement;
- a lack of clarity about the task;
- a sense of uneasiness about how it's going;
- a sense of being bruised by a recent encounter;
- a self-criticism because of a sense of failure;
- a mixture of positives and negatives;
- a sense of lacking skill in some area;
- difficult questions.

You could add to this list. The one leading the team meeting must attempt to hold in tension the three elements: task, individual and group, all of which need attention at different moments.

MLTs will soon find a variety of ways of starting meetings, but two possibilities are these:

1 Simply invite each person to say what they've brought with them out of the day's events and experiences.

2 Take 'a temperature reading' either in the whole group or in threes or pairs. To do this you move, at whatever speed you choose, through five separate stages of information giving. This is a listening, not a problem-solving process. The five stages are:

> **1** affirmations – find something positive to say to others;
>
> **2** new information – what's your news today?
>
> **3** puzzles – what do you want explaining, or need to know?
>
> **4** complaints and solutions – what's bugging you about who or what? What positive proposal do you have?
>
> **5** dreams, hopes and visions – what do you want?

Adapt, explore and borrow new ways of building the team – refuse to limit yourselves.

Purpose of the regular meeting

If the purpose of the meeting includes the following, what approach could you make to each one?

66 I tell you: one must still have chaos in one, to give birth to a dancing star. 99
FRIEDRICH NIETZSCHE IN DIARMUID O'MURCHU (1997B)

66 God's love for the steadfast heart. 99
PSALM 5

66 under his wings you will find refuge. 99
PSALM 9

- building **trust**;
- clarifying **vision** and **values**;
- recognizing the **differences** in the team and parish;
- knowing more about the **local context**;
- understanding **strengths** and **weaknesses**;
- **leading** the ministry of the **whole** congregation;
- helping to realize the church's **mission statement**;
- ensuring that the church is there **for the whole community**.

There are other purposes you could add.

Twelve Characteristics of Successful Teams
Check your Team against this list that has come out of the long experience of Derrick Rowland:

- teams develop and agree aims to which the whole team is committed;
- these aims are precise and understood by all members;
- team members show their respect for one another by actively listening to what is said and observing what is done;
- teams get things done better than individuals;
- individuals feel cared for, valued and understood;
- team members go out of their way to support and encourage others' activities;
- helpful feedback is normal;
- there is frequent review of how the team is doing as well as what it is doing, so the team continues to improve what it is and what it does;
- success is analysed so as to build upon it;
- the causes of mistakes are faced honestly so error is not repeated;
- hard decisions are taken;

66 I like the first few words of Isaiah 1.18 'Come now let us reason together, says the Lord'. For theological education to be viable and life producing, we have to come together and make sense of the situation we have before us. The best place to begin this life affirming endeavour is with ourselves. For theological education to be viable, life giving, life producing, and life affirming, I believe we have to begin by teaching ourselves and others the importance of spiritual intimacy. This knowledge will empower us to be accepting and respectful to each other's religious practices and when we find ourselves ministering among people of other cultures, all of us can meet at a middle point and together we can begin the birthing process, that is bringing forth new life. 99
THEODORA M. BROOKS

- individuals achieve well and are proud to be part of that team.

If it is the woman in the team who is always the one expected to sort out damaged relationships, it may be that the team needs to look at the underlying issues they are all working with, which may be unsaid, but very powerful.

What Learning Will Best Serve Local Ministry Leadership Teams and the Wider Local Ministry Vision?

As you will have already discovered, society at the end of the second millennium presents a complex learning situation. Adult Christians have an urgent need to learn discernment, openness and flexibility, with 'permission' to think and to reflect critically on the world, God's presence within it, and their opportunities for working with God in the world. By contrast, there is plenty of evidence of anxiety-driven control, authoritarianism, simplistic thinking and passivity surrounding issues of teaching and learning in the Church. There is a temptation for adult Christians to be submissive in the local church by giving up their power to those who offer fixed bodies of knowledge, and a hierarchy of teacher (who knows) and learner (an empty receptacle to be filled).

Learning for Ministry as Partnership needs to be more than induction to an agreed and protected body of knowledge, a watered-down version of traditional clergy or Reader training.

Learning implies risk and journeying – in partnership with others – leaving room for people to express normal feelings of impatience or anger or confusion. The trinitarian God of creativity, spontaneity, openness and discovery invites us to be open to being surprised, to learn new truths, and be arrested by wonder. The only kind of church worth working for, we suggest, is one which is becoming a learning community, with all its risks and genuine openness. This requires a fundamental attitude of partnership between clergy and laity and an end to all the inherited polarizations: adult/child, male/female, well-educated/incapable of thinking.

66 Within a Ministry Leadership Team, clergy and Readers have their important and distinctive expertise out of which they can draw for the benefit of all as does each team member from their work and experience. The self-confidence that laity so badly need is built up, as the culture gradually moves away from centring the church's life too much in the clergy. 99
ROBIN GREENWOOD

54

The core agenda for this learning is the desire to be an ever-deeper spiral of participation in God's life in the world, through trust, vulnerability, perseverance, responsibility and reflection, commitment to action, integration and honesty.

Your MLT and PCC, with the help of your facilitators, need to keep returning to such questions as:

1 What is the best learning for all to discern God at work in the world and to pursue their vocation as a church that works for the final purposes of God with the world – the Kingdom of God?

2 How can you create live and genuine forms of ministry and mission in community that are earthed and flourishing in the whole of life?

3 How can study for Local Ministry be about growth, deepening and moving away from fear which displaces love (1 John 4.18), through spiritual formation for all?

4 How can you ensure your theology has to do with everything – health, ecology, politics, economic matters, law and territory, as well as the person, family and gender?

Educational process for Ministry Leadership Teams is critically about discipleship and community formation. It's much deeper than training – 'this love re-invades us, shifts the boundaries of our being' (Micheal O'Siadhail).

As Ministry as Partnership is about the invitation to inhabit a tradition that brings life in all its fullness, there will need to be:

1 A move away from learning in blocks, with their danger of isolating reflection, and learning, from continuing ministry.

2 Purpose-built models of training for clergy or readers – not borrowed from inherited models. Within a MLT, clergy and Readers have their important and distinctive expertise out of which they can draw for the benefit of all. The purpose of the team learning process is for the team as a body to be reflecting on practice so that they can be effective and healthy in their task of resourcing the whole people of God in the local church. The team

> 66 The most serious danger is that this movement becomes inward-looking. This is a deep threat to the integrity of the vision, which is about the whole people of God sharing in the mission that God has entrusted to them. 99
> DAVID DURSTON

EZEK. 18.30–32

2 COR. 5.18–19

MATT. 5.18; 13.52; 21.31; 22.37–39; 23.8

together needs to return frequently to such questions as, 'What does our belief about God say about this?' and 'How is this God's life in the world?' So the self-confidence that laity so badly need as the culture gradually moves away from centring the Church's life too much in the clergy, is built up.

Instead of insisting on intense and prolonged stints of education preceding ministry, the theological under-standing of a Ministry Leadership Team should be developed naturally in tandem with what is going on. In this way there is a good chance of opening people up for new possibilities of celebrating the presence of God and learning the ways of accountability in ways that are interwoven with the practice of ordinary lives.

> 66 Help us to be always hopeful gardeners of the Spirit who know that without darkness nothing comes to birth, as without light nothing flowers. 99
> MAY SARTON

> 66 In our contemporary culture, our capacity to relate symbolically and imaginatively is poorly developed; we have become too individualistic, literalist, rational, logical and clinical. We have largely lost our capacity to dream, to imagine, to be playful, to celebrate, to ritualize, and being thus impoverished, we have lost our capacity to relate holistically. A rediscovery of meaningful ritual and inspirational sacrament is one of the more urgent needs of our time, a prerequisite for rediscovering an authentic sense of human, planetary and global community. 99
> DIARMUID O'MURCHU

A possible framework: four desirable strands

Facilitated team meetings

The MLT needs to meet regularly to address its task, team building, and for the mutual support of members.

Specialist training

Members will need to provide for themselves and others occasions which raise levels of competence and awareness in particular skills, e.g. children's work, supporting ministry at work, worshipping and preparation for sacraments. Some of this could be linked with diocesan, area or deanery training programmes. MLT learning needs to be passed on to the whole congregation.

Residential and day events

Experience elsewhere points to the value of bringing together several teams from differing contexts to study and pray around a common theme. Apart from direct learning, these can be occasions for much interaction between those from differing contexts and traditions united in a common faith.

Learning through reflection on baptismal and eucharistic living

If a MLT is to be a means for an awakening of church that can belong to every baptized person, its membership will be extremely varied – in age, in cultures and in educational experience. The group has no ideal point to reach educationally and so needs a continuing process for reflection which will strengthen and deepen its corporate work.

> 66 It is not the Church that makes the Eucharist, but rather quite the reverse: the Eucharist makes the Church. 99
> JOHN ZIZIOULAS

Suppose we begin by taking the shape or spine of the Holy Communion Service – which the ecumenical liturgical movement has made explicit to most churchgoers, if they were to stop and think about it for a moment. Imagine taking the key points of the liturgy in order as a syllabus or agenda over a period of a year – and repeating the process each year. At each point – say penitence, Gospel reading, intercession, peace, sharing of the bread and wine, the blessing, dismissal – everyone could have something to contribute because each person's experience of the Eucharist is of value and can be the basis for wider reflection. Imagine a whole set of issues, questions and interests impacting together:

> 66 Anyone who has been crucified and buried with Christ has been 'made like to' him (Rom. 6.5) and has 'put him on' as a garment (Gal. 3.27), and is also to 'walk according to his Spirit' (ROM. 8.5). 99

- to the particularities of space, time and personality in the local context;

- to recent experience in ministry;

- to the season of the calendar;

- to contemporary events;

- to memories of local events;

- to parts of the Christian tradition recalled by members of the group;

> 66 Every Christian is called and enabled to bear witness to him. 99
> 1 COR. 1.4–9

- to disciplined ways of interpreting life known to group members;

- to experiences of God's love in worship, prayer and daily living;

- to the needs of individuals.

Figure 12 is associated with this. At each point in the order of the Holy Communion (Eucharist) the MLT could

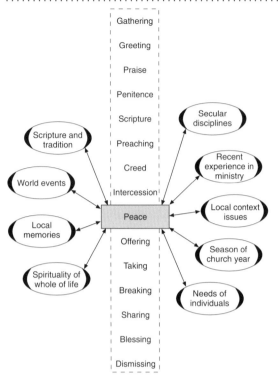

Figure 12 Using the various stages of the eucharist – word and sacrament – for reflective learning.

reflect together on many issues. The example given is focussed at the peace. It could equally well focus on any of the other stages.

Local Ministry can help churches become learning communities

If we are inviting laity as a whole to see themselves as on the front line in mission and ministry, in world and church, they need appropriate resourcing.

A learning community, rather than working at reactive problem solving, fosters radical questioning, review, and receiving outside information and feedback.

As you reflect on the learning available to your MLT, ministry teams and the whole church, ask what evidence is there that it is:

• often too safe and remote;

66 … our theological reflection must be rooted in and complemented by worship, prayer and meditation. We need to share in the life of the community of faith. We need to be open to the mystery of God's actions through worship and prayer. Like those who experienced the outpouring of the Holy Spirit on Pentecost, we too must be open to the actions of God. 99

TOM FITZGERALD

58

- takes the widest context of the triune God's saving activity in every place in every age;

- keeps connectedness with current international issues?

A key to this might be in recalling that the trinitarian profession of faith is not only the summing up of the revelation of the mystery of God, it is also the concrete *exposition of the hiddenness and unknowability of God.*

Consulting human experience is an identifying mark of virtually all contemporary theology. Increasingly, we need to understand how different peoples and communities have travelled in particular ways for reasons which are both very personal and also to do with the *Zeitgeist*, what is happening throughout the world of thought.

Human suffering adds a sharper edge to this doctrine of divine hiddenness.

Consider:

- Jewish reflection on the European holocaust.

- Liberation Theology's search for God in situations of extreme poverty and violence.

- Your own local experience here – how does suffering shape faith and theology?

In your learning processes check that you are listening to:

1 the questions and struggles of the people of a place at a particular time

2 the value systems and deepest hopes which give theology indispensible clues for revising received interpretations and arriving at new insights, e.g. the lived experience of:

    oppressed ethnic minorities;

    the marginalized position of women;

    abused children;

    laity in the church.

So we learn to reflect on the oppressed self as God's good gift – a deeply religious as well as human event.

In each case we can then ask its significance in terms of:

- spirituality,

- ethical values,

> ❝ Living trinitarian life means living as Jesus Christ lived; preaching the gospel; relying totally on God; offering healing and reconciliation; rejecting laws or customs and conventions that place persons beneath rules; resisting temptation; praying constantly; eating with modern-day lepers and other outcasts; embracing the enemy and the sinner; dying for the sake of the gospel if it is God's will. ❞
> CATHERINE MOWRY LACUGNA

> ❝ And God saw everything that he had made, and behold it was very good (Gen. 1.31). Only in the light of the eschatological consummation may this be said of our world as it is in all its confusion and pain. But those who may say it in spite of the suffering of the world, honour and praise God as their Creator.
>
> The verdict 'very good' does not apply simply to the world of creation in its state at any given time. It is true, rather, of the whole course of history in which God is present with his creatures in incursions of love that will finally lead it through the hazards and sufferings of finitude to participation in his glory. ❞
> WOLFHART PANNENBERG

> We are shepherded by the Lord.
PS. 23

> God's people have a leader in the wilderness.
EXOD. 13.18

> where two or three of you are gathered together in my name, there am I in the midst of them.
MATT. 18.20

> The Kingdom of God isn't there for the sake of the Church. The Church is there for the sake of the Kingdom. So – as we have said at the very beginning – all the Church's own concerns and interests must be subordinated to Jesus' concern for God's Kingdom. The Church's concern is not the Church. It is more than that. The Church has to do with God and his future for all men and women. It has to do with the new creation of all things for eternal life.
JÜRGEN MOLTMANN

- the words we use to articulate doctrine,

- how it is already bringing about new articulations of the divine mystery.

In particular, how does learning for Local Ministry help the church to see how to hold together in rich synthesis those things which might previously have been seen as opposites or alternatives:

self	other
matter	spirit
passion	intellect
embodiment	self-transcendence
nurturing	challenging
altruism	self-affirmation
receptivity	activity
love	power
being	doing
private	public
human	role
humanity	earth

MLTs should be able to signal that your church is committed to life-long learning for everyone, personally and corporately. It is in learning from our experience of living out faith in the everyday, that we are finding out who we are with God; and the kind of church and ministry we become, or choose to remain, speaks of our God.

Checking through this list and adding your own points too, notice how choices about public worship both limit and release our sense of God and God's ways with the world:

1 in the strands of Old/New Testament we emphasize;

2 in the stories we tell of church community;

3 in the commands we read off urgently from the tradition;

4 in the hymns we write and choose to sing;

5 in the physical ways we relate to one another in worship;

6 in the space we give for both anger and lament as well as praise;

7 in the metaphors for the divine mystery that especially work for us.

How far does your learning for everyone touch on the following?

- spiritual growth and development;
- being collaborative;
- exercising different models of leadership;
- strengthening quality of mind;
- stretching a sense of vocation;
- drawing out pastoral ability;
- inviting greater flexibility.

Finally, discuss this proposition:

Learning implies risk and journeying – in partnership with others. The trinitarian God of creativity, spontaneity, openness and discovery invites us to be open to being surprised, learn new truth, and be arrested by wonder. The only kind of Church worth working for is one which is becoming a learning community, with all its risks and genuine openness. This requires a fundamental attitude of partnership between clergy and laity and an end to all the inherited polarizations: adult/child, male/female, well-educated/incapable of thinking. The core agenda for this learning is the desire to be an ever deeper spiral of participation in God's life in the world through trust, vulnerability, perseverance, responsibility and reflection, commitment to action, integration and honesty.

Robin Greenwood and Caroline Pascoe

66 If you have built castles in the air, your work need not be lost; that is where they should be. Now put the foundation under them. 99
HENRY DAVID THOREAU

Ordained Local Ministry in the Team?

This handbook has assumed that all Christians have a vocation. We are all called – called to serve God at home, at work, in the neighbourhood and in and through the church. The varieties of service are 'ministry'. A tiny minority are called to ordained service: most are called to lay service. Whether ordained or lay, all share in Christian ministry, partners with each other in the service of God's Kingdom.

Ordained Local Ministry grows from this belief that all are called to ministry. Local churches, in which ordained and lay Christians are already sharing ministry and which have a Ministry Leadership Team (or whatever equivalent) ask themselves whether God is calling any of their members to Ordained Ministry in their own parishes.

In your group, considering the mission of your parish now, have you sufficient ministries of encouragement and leadership?

Imagine that in your church you've had the benefit of a Ministry Leadership Team for two years or more. Hopefully the Bishop will have publicly commissioned your parish as having a Ministry Leadership Team whose membership will continue to develop over the years. A periodic review of Local Ministry will have helped you see how the team itself and others in the local church have been:

- growing in their knowledge of God;

- personally discovering what their baptism means;

- accepting, with others, responsibility for local mission and ministry;

- learning to work together in ways that express commitment;

❝ Total Ministry is not a programme nor a system but a way of being, an attitude, a culture. ❞
STEWART ZABRISKIE

❝ Now you are the body of Christ and individually members of it. ❞
1 COR. 12.27

❝ you lack no spiritual gift. ❞
1 COR. 1.1–7

❝ listen to what the Spirit is saying to the churches. ❞
REV. 2.7

- persisting through thick and thin;

- bringing about changes to familiar patterns in parish life;

- building up others in worship, prayer and commitment to mission;

- training all the baptized in ministries for daily life and the local area;

- working with the church council through dialogue in decision-making;

- drawing out concern for others from the whole church;

- practising ways of working that are local, shared and empowering;

- becoming more attentive and responsible;

- meeting for support and training;

- deepening the level of encounter in your church's life;

- learning how very different people can work together and a great deal more.

The MLT will have grown through the training of all its members in reflection on their work as well as in enhancing particular skills. This handbook envisages that the ongoing learning will be rooted in the local context except where the team meets for training with other teams or regionally with those from other churches exercising youth, music, pastoral or teaching ministries. Regular experiential training in how to work together effectively and constructively as a team will be leading to developing and changing patterns of team-working. Through the rhythm of meeting, praying and reflecting together, leadership, contextual discernment, believing, living and witnessing to God in the world will all be deepening for the satisfaction of the MLT and the benefit of the whole church.

Reviewing and Looking Ahead

Use the following checklist to discuss how the role of the stipendiary priest has been stretching and changing. How honest can you be with one another about aspects that feel both positive and negative?

- developing with others and holding a vision of collaboration for all;
- affirming existing lay ministries and encouraging learning at many levels;
- discerning latent gifts and encouraging them;
- working with deanery/local training programmes;
- setting up and fostering the processes by which team members are discerned;
- making their own significant contribution to preparing for, teaching about and selecting the MLT as part of the wider Local Ministry pattern;
- meeting regularly with the MLT and others for prayer and learning together;
- co-ordinating and evoking the ministries of others;
- increasingly negotiating the range of responsibilities for the MLT and other groups that were formerly the preserve of clergy.

There will have been times when you'll have felt energized and transformed in your mission and ministry and times when you've lost direction and hope. But here you are, two years on. It's time that in the natural course of ministerial review in the diocese the MLT's work will have been fully included by the Bishop. The church council to whom the MLT is accountable will also need to review and set goals for a further period. Will you need some outside consultation from the diocese or a consultant? This evaluation process will have given you some new pointers and encouragement. It's time to review your facilitators – how is that working out for you and for them? Is it time for a change, or is stability what you need just now? It's a good time to celebrate and share your story with other churches and to listen to theirs. Or you may have serious problems – perhaps too few people caught the original vision, a decision was pushed too fast, there is mistrust and the need to rethink before moving on. Or you may be about to have changes in the staffing of your church through the moves of clergy or other licensed workers. Plan carefully to build new confidence in the whole church. In something as radically

❝ All members of the believing community, ordained and lay, are interrelated. On the one hand, the community needs ordained ministers … On the other hand, the ordained ministry has no existence apart from the community. Ordained ministers can fulfil their calling only in and for the community. They cannot dispense with the recognition, the support and the encouragement of the community.

They may appropriately be called priests because they fulfil a particular priestly service by strengthening and building up the royal and prophetic priesthood of the faithful through word and sacraments, through their prayers of intercession and through their pastoral guidance of the community.

Ordained ministers may be professional ministers in the sense that they receive their salaries from the church. The church may also ordain people who remain in other occupations or employment. ❞
WCC, LIMA TEXTS: MINISTRY SECTION

new as this, it would be amazing if mistakes were not made. This is all the more reason for having good support given by education, training and locally resourced ministries of support and encouragement.

You may find it helpful to review your MLT and all the groups that work with it through a consideration of the TASTE acronym from the Diocese of Christchurch in New Zealand – how far can you resonate with this?

Trust:
promoting a culture of belief in the local people's ability to organize their own ministry together.

Affirm:
valuing the good in the past and the present life of the congregation, and helping people give good feedback to each other.

Support:
helping put in place systems that foster ways of working together, especially in teams or pairs, and providing backup.

Train:
but not too much! All training is available to everyone and must be relevant.

Encourage:
each other, all the time.

Give yourselves some encouragement by creating an act of worship to mark where you've got to – warts and all! Members of the church council and MLT could do this together. Using your local resources plus anyone or anything that may be helpful – including your facilitators – create a special service. Invite lots of visitors – other local ministry churches, other local churches, friends from work and community, and members of the public and your neighbourhood, representatives of the wider church. Make an exhibition of your work and plans.

Give special attention to:

- The space to be used for the worship – use it thoroughly and flexibly.

- The planning group – select a wide spectrum of people and skills.

66 And only where the guides and leaders of the churches are themselves trustworthy and stake their lives on what they do will 'people of God' follow them. That is why it can be said that the church must constantly be reborn. Unless the 'people of God' allow themselves to be incorporated into God's building as living stones, there will be no temple, no view from any prospect, no place to which we can look to find God. 99
ANTON HOUTEPEN

66 Knowing God's love gives us boldness. 99
EPH. 3.12–21

- The resources – texts, music, voices, sensations.

- The balance between sound and silence.

- The most appropriate timing.

Have a party to show that Local Ministry helps churches and communities to know their true selves in sharing and celebration.

In terms of the ministries you need – is the make-up of your MLT well balanced?

The overall question for the local church now is whether your MLT has sufficient leadership and support. For example, it may be clear that a link is missing to some new or important aspect of the church's ministry. Or God might be calling one or several members of the Ministry Leadership Team to ordination – unpaid and regionally selected. You may react to this second suggestion in many ways – including the following, and no doubt others:

- we've already got a vicar/priest/ordained minister;

- I thought Local Ministry was getting away from depending on clergy;

- yes, there's something missing in our team's work;

- we've got enough clergy thank you very much;

- it would relieve pressure on our vicar because we have several churches;

- it would give us a vicar of our own rather than sharing with other parishes in our area;

- yes, but at least we can get rid of laity on the team if it's not working.

Part of your answer to the question of Ordained Local Ministry will depend on your circumstances. What is envisaged as possible or allowable by your wider church setting?

Spend as much time as you need discussing the principles of the Nevada Total Ministry Programme. How do you respond? Where do you agree or disagree?

❝ Very simply, we may ask whether our institutions, rituals and administrative practices foster elitism, discrimination, competition, or any of several 'archisms', or whether the church is run like God's household: a domain of inclusiveness, interdependence and co-operation, structured according to the model of *perichoresis* among persons. ❞
CATHERINE MOWRY LACUGNA

❝ If it ever comes about that 'a clergyman' is a man who takes services on Sundays but does not touch the lives of the people otherwise, it would change the whole character of the Church of England ... and the change would not be for the better. ❞
F. R. BARRY

Nevada Total Ministry Programme

- Each congregation is to be a 'ministering community' rather than a community gathered around a minister, sufficient in ministry from within its own membership, including local deacons and priests wherever possible.

- Each member of the church will have the opportunity to serve our Lord in church and world, through ministries, which will vary greatly, according to gifts, available time and opportunity.

- Seminary-trained clergy and laity will increasingly be trainers, enablers, supervisors and pastors of trainees.

- Congregations will become less dependent on seminary-trained people as doers of ministry.

- The diocese, as the primary unit of interdependence in the life of the church, is the support system. The diocese will provide training and support for the various forms that ministry can take, including local priests and deacons.

(In the USA, seminary refers to residential theological training.)

There are no blueprints because every context makes different demands. For a discussion of 'local' see Chapter 1 of 'Stranger in the Wings.' Advisory Board of Ministry Policy Paper No. 8, 1998.

The point is, if these are the questions and principles being worked out over there, what questions and opportunities does that raise for us here? What would we certainly want to avoid! All the time you need to be asking how local is local for us? Is the vicar of two or five parishes local enough? And how would the combination of locally ordained and lay work within our MLT resource our mission and ministry?

A key element in the discussion of Ordained Local Ministry is the recognition that if we are to resonate with the earliest patterns of Christian ministry and community practice, there can be no question of local ordination in isolation from a ministry team that exists to enable the mission and ministry of the whole of the local church.

66 Despite a long history of stipendiary ministry in rural and remote areas, adequate formation of the whole Church has not occurred. The authorized leader of a local community mirrors the community to itself. Thus a priest grows into being a eucharistic person, a person of thanksgiving, deeply sensitive to the holiness of all life, and perceptive of the ordinariness of God in the local context. 99
BRIAN FARRAN

66 for most of Christian history, and for much of English history too, there has been a close link between the local settlement, the local congregation and the local priest. 'Local' priesthood is not therefore a new invention, but it may perhaps be seen as a recovery of healthy rootedness. 99
STRANGER IN THE WINGS

333

For a major reconsideration of patterns of ministry over the century, revealing the immense variety in differing localities, see *A Case for Change* and *The Church with a Human Face* by Edward Schillebeeckx, and Nathan Mitchell's *Mission and Ministry*.

The Right of a Community to a Priest

Just as there can be no priest without community, you can argue the right of a community to a priest. Every group using this handbook will have its own slight nuances about language and expectations of clergy. There will be differences of view within the historically defined traditions – Anglican, Methodist, Roman Catholic and so on. Is there for you an intrinsic link between a local church often celebrating the Eucharist (Word and Sacrament) as a key way of nourishing all its people for mission and ministry in world and church? Do you see the role of presiding as one you would always or normally associate as part of the role of an ordained person? If so, how do your reconcile the need for the church to be engaged in mission and ministry supported by the Eucharist with the availability of a priest in your setting? You may have one or more ordained persons in your community or you may share a priest with another or several other churches.

Some churches prefer to celebrate the Eucharist only occasionally – which can be a sign of the high value they place upon it. If your church accepts the principle that the Eucharist is the heart of community of Christians (Word and Sacrament), it will make theological and pastoral nonsense if a local community is regularly prevented from celebrating Holy Communion. What is lost when a priest simply comes for an hour to make that celebration 'valid' or when the elements of bread and wine are brought from a service elsewhere?

Discuss in the group how far it makes sense to speak in terms of the right of every local church to be capable of doing all that is necessary to realize its aim of becoming **a community of disciples of Jesus** and as such to be constantly growing.

> In canon 6 of the Council of Chalcedon (451) we see a fundamentally ecclesial conception of the ministry. The concept of *ordinatio* comprises not only the laying on of hands by a 'bishop' with the prayer of the whole community to the Spirit, but also, if it is to be valid, the calling and appointing by a particular Christian community. The community calls; *this* is the 'priestly vocation'. The community knows it has the right to pastors or leaders. Leo the Great says: 'He who must preside over all must be chosen by all'. What is at stake here is the reciprocity between the community and the ministry.
> EDWARD SCHILLEBEECKX IN GROLLENBERG

Do you accept that, for the sake of catholicity, a built-in limitation is the requirement that each local community be in union with, and subject to, the criticism of other local churches?

What do you really believe about priesthood or ordained ministry? Allow for a wide range of deeply held views. To stretch your thinking, encourage one or two in the group to read either *Transforming Priesthood. A New Theology of Mission and Ministry*, or *Practising Community*, both by Robin Greenwood. In both these books there is a real attempt to show how the priest is not simply the one who can preside at the Eucharist, while by definition others cannot. The question is opened up of how far a local church, working for God's Kingdom here and now, needs someone set apart to ensure that through the ministries of all, that community is being built up, led, and linked with all other churches. In the group, as you explore ordained ministry as linked with the life and purpose of the local church, try using the following outline on which to hang you own thoughts:

The parish priest (or whatever language you want to work with) is one called by God, by the Bishop (regional leader and focus of unity) and by the people, and has a sense of inner call to preside and exercise oversight, within and for the local church:

- In terms of **discernment** – knowing and helping all to know the neighbourhood, the christian tradition(s) and how best to help them engage with each other.

- In terms of **blessing** – to be assured and bring assurance of God's grace in the ministries of all, to encourage and sustain new initiatives as well as to warn and to safeguard the community when there are signs that the Kingdom is not being well served.

- In terms of **witnessing** – alone sometimes, and often with others, to practise being a sign of God's Kingdom to those on the edge or in particular need; and also to build up all who will witness in their own right, from

66 Ministry for the kingdom of justice and peace. 99
LUKE 4.18–19

66 Episcope embraces the dimension of ministry which includes discerning and articulating a vision for a local congregation; enabling and bringing about change in communities; identifying restraints and dangers; resolving conflict and so on. The person exercising episcope does not do so simply by virtue of her or his office, simply by being there. The dimension of ministry is hands-on work requiring the development of a particular set of skills in which many clergy have not been intentionally formed and trained. 99
STEVEN CROFT

their own stories, to the saving presence of the triune God in the whole of the life of the world.

Expand and modify these points until you are as clear as you can be. (See Chapter 6 'The Presiding Ministry' in *Transforming Priesthood: A New Theology of Mission and Ministry* (1999) and Chapter 4 'Equal and Different Ministries' in *Practising Community: The Task of the Local Church* (1999) both by Robin Greenwood and published by SPCK, London.)

A national working party (1991) on ordained local ministry described priesthood as 'Representing Christ's presence in the world and among his people, seeking, feeding and serving his sheep, and representing Christ's people before God, praying for them and with them.'

The 1991 working party identified five aspects of Ordained Local Ministry. Discuss each in turn.

1 eucharistic presidency;

2 representing the universal church in the local setting;

3 challenging others to respond to their own baptismal vocation;

4 accepting a distinctive role in society;

5 receiving a legal status which binds priest, church and community in relationship.

How do you place these discussions in relationship to the theology of church referred to earlier in this handbook, especially the emphasis on a trinitarian understanding of God and the church's service of that triune God's mission for all creation?

Discuss together this quotation from the Lichfield Diocese Submission to the House of Bishops (1995):

From time to time, the Christian community is able to recognize in one of its members a charism of the holy Spirit which enables that person to be a special focus of the representative task that is the calling of all. The local church recognizes that such people embody and signal what it means for it to be the Church of God.

These people are in a real sense sacramental of the church's identity and ministry and, as such, have a distinct role to contribute to the formation and leadership of its ministry.

66 If we really want to reanimate life within the church, don't we have a duty to establish church as basic community among us? Can the tensions arising from this be worse than the deadly indifference we experience all too frequently now? 99
J. B. METZ

66 Every process of reinterpretation introduces elements which are wholly novel ... A traditional process of creative thought cannot be carried on without wholly new additions being made to existing tradition ... It is logically impossible for tradition to operate without the addition of wholly original interpretative judgements at every stage of transmission. 99

MICHAEL POLANYI IN AVIS

It has always seemed appropriate that those with this 'sacramental identity' should be set apart to preside at the church's Eucharist when its own identity as the community of Christ is most sharply displayed'.

Do you believe it is a distinctive role to represent, to teach, to build up and to lead? Are you clear why the church 'ordains' anyone?

Try completing the following sentence in up to 20 words. 'In our locality an Ordained Local Minister would ....
....'

Objections to Ordained Local Ministry

Naturally in the case of such a new development, there will be reasons why churches will approach this with extreme caution. Objections to OLM include the following. As you listen carefully to members of your church you will hear these – you may own some of them for yourselves as well as adding some new ones.

- It creates a third-rate priesthood.

- It undermines the laity.

- It just creates mass priests.

- It's impossible for a local priest to relate to everyone locally.

- It makes us look stupid when they move away.

- It'll be impossible to stop them moving into other clergy roles.

- It'll be possible to get stuck with a disastrous local priest, who doesn't go.

66 Amidst the vast scene of the world's problems and tragedies you may feel that your own ministry seems so small, so insignificant, so concerned with the trivial. What a tiny difference it can make to the world that you should run a youth club, or preach to a few people in a church, or visit families with seemingly small result. But consider: the glory of Christianity is its claim that small things really matter and that the small company, the very few, the one man, the one child are of infinite worth to God. Let that be your inspiration. 99

MICHAEL RAMSEY

What are the benefits of OLM that is truly collaborative and rooted in local teams?

This is a clear case of the local church needing to interweave its own story with the 2,000-year story of the followers of Jesus – in its kaleidoscope of variations.

Some of the vital ideas you will need to discuss are listed here:

1 How far does the Ministry Leadership Team of the local church need to include one who is specially called to a

representative role – and if you share a priest with several other places, is there a serious gap?

2 No public ministry of the church can truly operate in isolation. OLM without a team, just as MLT without its own priest, is incomplete.

So how local is local for you?

When the leadership and overseeing is held by all in partnership – on the basis that no one is actually called to be irresponsible – what difference does it make to the fears that a local priest would not be 'up to the mark' in terms of leadership, when an emphasis is made that no ministry works alone?

The church assembles at a specific place.
1 COR. 1.2, 12.5 AND 14.23

What exactly would you want to be the central focus of an OLM's ministry in your situation?

Is the person in fact already 'the president of the local Christian community'? Is this within a MLT or something approaching it? Do you have some team work to do first? This model assumes you need only one OLM in a local church – but never in isolation from the equal but different ministries of others – because leadership is being explored corporately.

The local church is not alone but dispersed throughout the world and beyond time.
EPH. 1.22, 2.22, 3.10, 5.22–33; COL. 1.18

Is your need focused more on the need for team leadership?

An obvious example of this would be when the vicar of several parishes recognizes that he or she cannot belong to more than one Ministry Leadership Team.

Are you looking for someone to hold the ring about directing, animating, guiding and inspiring the community – knowing that others will be part of this also? Care should be taken not to assume that the natural leader could automatically exercise a representative priestly role.

A definition of church used and developed over many generations.
MATT. 18.20

Is it part of your assumption that such a person needs to be an ordained person? Or are you looking for a team chaplain? This is to separate the leadership from the sacramental-person role. Someone other than the leader becomes the OLM and presides at the Eucharist. It could be more than one person. This ministry does not have to be restricted to sacramental aspects of the church's work.

Or would your OLM be assistant to the stipendiary priest in a team involving lay people as well; in not reinforcing the traditional model of 'helping the vicar'; in expressing a true partnership within a collaborative MLT?

So what kind of people should you be looking for?
People who are:

- local but open enough to the wider church and world;

- worshipping members of the local church;

- growing in faith with a story to tell of God's work in them;

- not necessarily of that place but committed to staying;

- clearly on a spiritual quest and able to support others on theirs;

- people of discernment, judgement and wisdom; ˙

- really interested in the flourishing of that neighbour-hood;

- able to relate to and like working with others;

- pastorally alert;

- flexible, adaptable, and open to change;

- gifted and skilled in particular ways.

Some key resources to stimulate your thinking:

'Stranger in the Wings: A Report on Local Non-Stipendiary Ministry', Advisory Board of Ministry Policy Paper No. 8.

'The Sign We Give', Report of the Roman Catholic Bishops of England and Wales.

This handbook endorses the Church of England regulations for OLM laid down in ABM Policy Paper No. 1.

The Calling Process
The selection of leaders within the New Testament churches combines a practice deriving from the Jewish tradition of throwing lots after prayer, and the discernment of the community of those with required skills to fulfil public roles. When you were planning to call

> 66 The journey of the soul through life is strangely like the progress of the child Alice through Looking-glass Land. Alice finds herself wandering through a strange, unstable world of circumstance, and undergoing many bewildering experiences which seem, as the experiences of our life often do, chaotic and unmeaning ... In spite of her bewilderment the child caught in the web of circumstance was never really lost; each baffling experience contributed something to the whole. The hand of the Player was hovering over the Pawn. 99
> EVELYN UNDERHILL IN WARD AND WILD

members of your MLT you had to recall the two poles of Christian vocation – the individual, like Samuel in the Temple (1 Sam. 3) or Amos or Hosea, and the community calling, like Matthias (Acts 1) and Stephen, Philip, Prochorus, etc. in Acts 6. A true calling will combine something of both these elements. In recent history we have placed most of the emphasis on the individual's sense of inner call; now is a time to remember the early church's pattern of calling people to ministries it needed to be filled.

One of the things that is important in local ministry is the understanding that we cannot rush the process. Before any call is issued by the local church there needs to be months of teaching to remind everyone in the congregation of their own gifts and responsibilities and to see how God is always drawing people on to new possibilities. This is important to dispel connections between calling and personal ideas about status, popularity, reward for service, alleviation of personal problems and so on. Explore again what the Bible has to say about being called to ministry – remembering both individual and community initiatives.

Criteria for Ordained Local Ministry

Those called as local priests need to have the potential – with training:

- to be representative of the people;

- to be an enthusiastic developer of the ministries of others;

- to be disinterested in clerical professional advancement;

- to be able to appreciate and fulfil the role of president – linking Eucharist with the mission and ministry of all;

- to be able to help the church interweave its long tradition with the needs of individuals and groups in church and neighbourhood;

- to be able to allow others to lead naturally as their skills are appropriate to situations;

- to be able to grow in pastoral effectiveness;

❝ Many respondents [to a survey] felt that they were not accepted as a 'proper' priest by other clergy – indeed, that they were 'second class'. Support from the incumbent was considered central to the LNSM's experience. Some respondents thought that other members of the church needed (re)training to work effectively with LNSMs. ❞
STRANGER IN THE WINGS

It'll be essential to have a written agreement with the local team as part of the licensing process.

The criteria and processes for selection, training, ordination and licensing will vary from diocese to diocese. Each diocese works within the boundaries of its contextual submission that is acceptable to the Ministry Division of the Archbiship's Council.

Issues that need to be addressed include:

1 the period for which a MLT must be functioning before considering OLM;

2 the sense of how healthy is the MLT at the present time;

3 the sense that OLM is seen as an integral part of the development of the MLT;

4 work with existing vocations officers and the diocesan director of ordinands;

5 who needs to take part in consultations – stipendiary clergy, PCC, MLT, facilitators, deanery officers and committees, vocations adviser, archdeacon, Bishop – and at what stages?

There are clear guidelines, reviewed periodically, for a Bishop's Selection Conference held locally, training, ordination and licensing, working agreements and continuing ministerial education, supervision and appraisal. What is clear is that all these processes provide new opportunities for integrating laity and clergy in a kaleidoscopic pattern that is built on a social trinitarian understanding of God.

The potential for Ordained Local Ministry, carefully thought through and well resourced locally and regionally, seems very high. It is possible for every local church – if they wish – to have an ordained member of their Ministry Leadership Team without expecting too much of a priest who may have many parishes. It is vital, however, to be clear that such a development of ministry is not a last-ditch attempt to keep up the inherited pattern of displacing lay ministry and encouraging dependency. Rather let OLM be a clear signal, through its partnership in ministry with a MLT, of the

66 Say 'yes' to joining the mission of God – to travelling hopefully to new and unexplored places in the company of those who want to be part of God's coming kingdom, that *shalom* which characterizes the triune God's final intention for all. This is to be knowingly subversive through the often costly creation of communities – focused on the cross of Christ – that work for God's good End.

Being led into the truth is a continuing and often painful saga which goes beyond the limits of past traditions, stirs churches to do things for the very first time, gives freedom for the Christian life to be sometimes a party, always discerning into the heart of things, and never complete. 99
ROBIN GREENWOOD

kind of church that recognizes and wants to develop the ministries of all God's people.

A True Partnership: Local and Wider Church Together

Most dioceses, through representative post holders in parishes, deaneries, resource departments and bishop's staff and council, are working creatively to identify and publicize their strategies for mission and ministry. One of the clear conclusions is that for a church that intends to undertake what is actually sustainable, as well as to challenge the culture of overwork, both radical prioritization and genuine commitment have to be constant features of life. What are the implications of Local Ministry as a strategy, rather than a scheme for just a few? Any Diocesan Working Group on Local Ministry exists not just to serve those parishes actively exploring a resource or handbook like this one, but to recognize the potential of deanery plans to be more than just a reshuffling of stipendiary posts to maintain the inherited patterns in which – for many reasons – clergy have so often displaced the proper ministries of all God's people. A Bishop's Council or its equivalent might consider asking itself:

1 What provision can be made for making a concise statement of ministerial strategy which takes into account the projected long-term reduction of numbers of stipendiary clergy, despite the current upturn in the number of those recommended for training; the increasing proportion of clergy who are non-stipendiary ministers; real evidence from recent questions asked of the parishes; statements by the Bishop, and the diocesan commitment to partnership in ministry in every respect?

2 What assurance is there that any body set up to explore or deliver developing education and training needs will be honoured and strengthened in its work through dialogue with the declared aims and objectives of the diocese in mission and ministry?

66 A Christian community is responsible, with the Bishop, for recognizing the spiritual gifts and needs of its members and for calling into service from its members the leaders it needs to be about its life and mission. Where needed, this appropriately involves the ordination of self-supporting, local leaders as deacons and priests. It is also required to share the Gospel message and life with its neighbouring communities not yet evangelized. Don't train the leaders too much; don't rely upon leadership from outside. And Christian community that is doing these things, no matters what its size, is fully the church. The Bishop's staff are crucial in supporting all of this. 99
ROLAND ALLEN

3 Can the formation and procedures of a Bishop's Council be adapted to act as a gearing system which constantly takes the pulse of the diocese through the interaction of knowledgeable representatives of key roles? In particular, on issues of ministry as partnership that must include at least: Bishop's staff, Finance Committee, Pastoral Committee, Resource Council, Area/Rural deans representative, Local Ministry Working Group, Education and Training Group, the Diocesan Director of Ordinands and Non-Stipendiary Ministry Officer, Diocesan Continuing Ministerial Education Officer, and the Ministry Development Officer or Director of Ministry.

3 What investigation and review processes does the Council require to ensure that the long-term energy required to change the ministerial paradigm is available and being targeted in the most helpful ways?

Finally – words of encouragement

As you take practical steps in the Local Ministry vision of the church, there will be setbacks and times when you might be tempted to give up. Take encouragement from the fact that your church is part of a world-wide Anglican and ecumenical movement led by the Spirit of God. Local Ministry or Total Ministry offers a structure to help discover ways of being the church that actively promotes the mission of the local church, sensitive to the particular needs and opportunities of every place, as the calling and responsibility of every baptized person working together.

Local Ministry describes the interaction of diverse gifts and ministries, accredited and unaccredited, of the whole people of God in the cause of God's purposes for all creation. Essentially, Local Ministry may be regarded as shorthand for the way the church in a given locality through laity and clergy in partnership take effective responsibility for living out God's life. As this is still not accepted everywhere as simply a normal aspect of being the church, there will be times when you feel isolated and alone. It is then that you need to revisit the vision and

66 Difference must be not merely tolerated, but seen as a fund of necessary polarities between which our creativity can spark like a dialectic. Only then does the necessity for interdependence become unthreatening. Only within that interdependency of different strengths, acknowledged and equal, can the power to seek new ways of being in the world generate ... Difference is that raw and powerful connection from which our personal power is forged. 99
AUDRE LORDE IN JOHNSON, ELIZABETH A.

strategy you have worked out together and in partnership with the wider church under the Spirit's guidance.

An essential purpose of Local Ministry is to help churches to become adult in their approach to the distribution of roles against the background of the richness of belonging to the church world-wide. Key to this is an eschatological approach to the mission of the local church which focuses the task of the local church to generate communities of disciples, who assume the interactive pattern given by our Lord to reveal the Gospel through relationships of mutuality and reconciliation.

So, in local worshipping, witnessing communities, the church can offer to society a partial portrait of what God has in mind for all human and created relationships, and at work with God in the world, can take a full and active part in the realization of foretastes of the Kingdom. It can hope to make the connection between these transforming patterns of ministry and the fundamental core of our hope of salvation. In vibrant, dynamic community, witnessing to the promise of redeemed sociality, it is revealed that the coming reign of God is not offered to us as individuals in isolation, but as the whole creation in qualities of relatedness which echo the indwelling mutuality which is the being of the triune God.

Through Local Ministry then, local worshipping communities are launching on journeys of discovery, energized by a developing, shared vision of more fully co-operating with God's vitality in the world. This is articulated through reflecting, imagining and extrapolating together to answer repeatedly – in differentiated repetition – the questions 'What is God calling us to here and now?' 'What does experience of involvement, tradition, story, memories, successes, challenges, wilderness, reveal to us about God at work through this particular ecclesiastical event or community?' 'What glimpses might we be shown of God's desires for our shared tomorrow?'

The potential and energy of transformative partnership for ministry derives from communities, who reveal in their own life and relationships the aliveness of the risen Lord, made available by the Spirit. The church is constituted by those who are capable of recognizing the

> 66 It was said, 'The church is going down the tubes.' A person's face broke out in a smile and he said, 'Yes! And have you imagined what it might look like as it comes out of the tubes?' We have a choice: which image will guide us as we look forward? Church history is the story of people re-imagining the church and ministry, in tension with those who would make it a graven image. The Hebrew people were called into a covenant to be a pilgrim people rather than an idolatrous people. The option for the future is clearly to adventure with God, a celebrational slide in the spirit of joy, love and peace down the tubes into God's ever unfolding future. 99
> PAUL DYER

66 'Teacher, order your disciples to stop.' He answered, 'I tell you, if these were silent, the stones would shout out!' 99

LUKE 19.39–40

Lord as Jesus of Nazareth and the Spirit of that Jesus working among them. This church reproduces itself as she initiates others collectively into seeing the Lord.

Local Ministry assists churches to know themselves as communities of the resurrection and crucibles of the Spirit. It encourages them to build up the confidence of clergy and laity together. Local Ministry can help the whole church see a new threshold to being confident as cross-shaped, vulnerable and healthy Christian communities, committed to witness to the life of the God who is three and one, so helping the whole of humanity share in God's mission for all creation.

References and Further Reading

Adam, David, *The Open Gate, Celtic Prayers for Growing Spiritually*, London, Church Information Office, 1985.

Advisory Board of Ministry, 'Local NSM: The Report of a Church of England Working Party Concerned with Local Non-Stipendiary Ministry', ABM Paper No. 1, London, 1991.

Advisory Council for the Church's Ministry (ACCM), 'Education For the Church's Ministry: The Report of the Working Party on Assessment' Occasional Paper No. 22, London, 1987.

Alberigo, Giuseppe and Gutierriez, Gustav (eds), 'Where does the Church Stand?' *Concilium*, Edinburgh, T. & T. Clark, 1981.

'All are Called: Towards a Theology of the Laity', London, Church House Information Office, 1985.

Augustine, *De Trinitate*, vii, 12.14, in Jürgen Moltmann, *The Trinity and the Kingdom of God*, London, SCM, 1980.

Avegard, Ian and Muir, David, *Fit for the Purpose. The Meaning of Christian Vocation and How to Respond When God Calls*, St John's, Nottingham, 1997.

Avis, Paul, *Authority, Leadership and Conflict in the Church*, London, Mowbray, 1992.

Baez, Joan, in Taubman, Stan, 1994.

Barry, F. R. *Asking the Right Questions: Church and Ministry*, London, Hodder & Stoughton, 1960.

Barth, Karl, *Against the Stream*, London, SCM, 1954.

Behr-Sigel, Elizabeth, in Grey, Mary C., 1997.

Behrens, James, *Practical Church Management. A Guide for Every Parish*, Leominster, Gracewing, 1998.

Bishops' Conference of England and Wales, *The Sign We Give*, Chelmsford, Matthew James Publishing Ltd, 1995.

Board of Education, *Called to be Adult Disciples*, London, General Synod, 1987.

Board of Mission, *A Time for Sharing: Collaborative Ministry in Mission*, London, 1995.

Boff, Leonardo, *Trinity and Society*, London, Burns & Oates, 1992.

Bondi, Richard, *Leading God's People. Ethics for the Practice of Ministry*, Abingdon Press, 1989.

Borgeson, Josephine and Wilson, Lynne (eds), *Reshaping Ministry: Essays in Memory of Wesley Frensdorff*, Jethro Publications, 1990.

Brooks, Theodora M., 'Spiritual Intimacy and its Impact on Theological Education', *Ministerial Formation*, Geneva, WCC, January 1998.

Brueggemann, Walter, *Old Testament Theology*, Minneapolis, Fortress, 1992.

—— *Theology of the Old Testament, Testimony, Dispute, Advocacy*, Minneapolis, Fortress, 1997.

Carroll, Lewis, *Alice Through the Looking Glass*, Puffin, 1998.

Cassidy, Sheila, *Good Friday People*, London, Darton, Longman and Todd, 1991.

Christifideles Laici, (simplified version), Pinner, The Grail, 1989.

Chung Hyun Kyung, in Grey, Mary C., 1997.

Clark, David (ed.), *Changing World, Unchanging Church?* London, Mowbray, 1997.

Crawford, J. and Kinnamon, M., in Graham, Elaine, 1996.

Croft, Steven, *Ministry in Three Dimensions. Ordination and Leadership in the Local Church*, London, Darton, Longman and Todd, 1999.

Dearborne, Tim, in Hill, Mike, *Reaching the Unchurched*, Amersham-on-the-Hill, Scripture Press, 1994.

Doohan, Leonard, *The Lay-Centred Church: Theology and Spirituality*, Minneapolis, Winston Press, 1984.

Dulles, Avery, *Models of the Church*, Dublin, Gill & Macmillan, 1974.

Dussel, Enrique, *Ethics and the Theology of Liberation*, Maryknoll, 1978; and in Walton, Martin, 1994.

Durston, David and Richter, Philip, *New Fire*, Diocese of Salisbury, 1999.

Dyer, Paul, 'The Discovery of Baptismal Ministry – Reflections on a Pilgrimage to Understanding', in *Growing Mutual Ministry in New Zealand*, Anglican Church of Aotearoa New Zealand and Polynesia, 1997.

Eastman, Theodore A., *The Baptising Community*, New York, The Seabury Press, 1982.

Etchells, Ruth, *Set My People Free: A Lay Challenge to the Churches*, London, Fount, 1995.

Farran, Brian, *Leadership. Resources to Help Your Congregation Become a Ministering Community*, Kalgoorlie, Diocese of Perth, 1996.

Fernandez, Eleazar S., 'Sharing in Ministerial Formation and Laos', *Ministerial Formation*, Geneva, WCC, January 1998.

Fitzgerald, Tom, *Pentecost and Theological Education in Ministerial Formation*, Geneva, WCC, 1999.

Ford, David F. (ed.), *Essentials of Christian Community*, Edinburgh, T. & T. Clark, 1996.

—— *Why Church?* Society for the Study of Theology Paper, 1998, available from Centre for the Study of Theology, Essex University, Colchester.

Fung, Raymond, *The Isaiah Vision*, Geneva, WCC, 1992.

Galbraith, Douglas, in Northcott, Michael, 1998.

Graham, Elaine L., *Transforming Practice, Pastoral Theology in an Age of Uncertainty*, London, Mowbray, 1996.

Greenwood, Robin, *Practising Community: The Task of the Local Church*, London, SPCK, 1996 (1999).

Greenwood, Robin, *Transforming Priesthood: A New Theology of Mission and Ministry*, London, SPCK, 1994 (1999).

Greenwood, Robin and Pascoe, Caroline, *Learning for Local Ministry*, unpublished paper, 1998.

Grey, Mary C., *Beyond the Dark Night: A Way Forward for the Church?* London, Cassell, 1997.

Grollenberg, Lucas and others, *Minister? Pastor? Prophet? Grass Roots Leadership in the Churches*, London, SCM, 1980.

Gunton, Colin, *The Promise of Trinitarian Theology*, Edinburgh, T. & T. Clark, 1991.

Gutierrez, Gustavo, *We Drink From Our Own Wells: The Spiritual Journey of a People*, London, SCM, 1984.

—— *The God of Life*, London, SCM, 1984.

Hardy, Daniel W., *God's Ways With the World: Thinking and Practising Christian Faith*, Edinburgh, T. & T. Clark, 1996.

—— *Local Ministry*, A paper given at the Lambeth Conference Marketplace, July 1998. Available through the Edward King Institute, Local Ministry Office, 4 College Green, Gloucester.

Hardy, Daniel W. and Ford, David F., *Jubilate: Theology in Praise*, London, DLT, 1984.

Hawkins, Thomas R., *The Learning Congregation: A New Vision of Leadership*, Louisville, John Knox Press, 1997.

Hildegarde of Bingen in O'Murchu, Diarmuid, 1997.

Hollis, Crispin, in Grey, Mary C., 1997.

Honey, Peter, *Twelve Watercolours of Bibury*, Maidenhead, 1998.

House of Bishops, *Eucharistic Presidency: A Theological Statement*, London, Church House Publishing, 1997.

Houston, Gaie, *The Red Book of Groups and How to Lead Them Better*, The Rochester Foundation, 1993.

Houtepen, Anton, *People of God: A Plea for the Church*, London, SCM, 1984.

Hurley, Michael, *Transforming Your Parish. Building a Faith Community*, Dublin, The Columba Press, 1998.

International Symposium on Local/Total/Common Ministry in San Francisco (1999): Web Site http://maffin.net/june/totalministry.htm.

Johnson, Elizabeth A., *She Who Is: The Mystery of God in Feminist Theological Discourse*, New York, Crossroad Herder, 1998.

Jung, C. G., *Psychology and Alchemy, Collected Works*, vol. 12, William McGuire (exec. ed.) 2nd edn; rsd, London, Routledge & Keegan Paul, 1953 (1968).

Kaspar, Walter, *The God of Jesus Christ*, New York, Crossroad, 1984.

Kilroy, Bernard, 'Beyond the Dark Night: A Way Forward for the Church', in *Ministry*, Journal of the Edward King Institute for Ministry Development, vol. 2, no. 2, Autumn 1998.

King, Philip, 'Leading a Church', *Administry*, vol. 1, no. 6, 1997.

LaCugna, Catherine Mowry, *God for Us: The Trinity and Christian Life*, New York, Harper, 1991.

Leech, Kenneth, *The Sky is Red. Discerning the Spirit of the Times*, London, Darton, Longman & Todd, 1997.

Leonard, Ann, in Clark, David, 1997.

Lossky, Vladimir, *The Image and Likeness of God*, London, Mowbray, 1975.

Lowen, Alexander, in Taubman, Stan, 1994.

MacIntyre, Alastair, in Leech, Kenneth, 1997.

Marsh, Thomas A., *Gift of Community: Baptism and Confirmation*, Delaware, Michael Glazier, 1984.

McPartlan, Paul, *The Eucharist Makes the Church*, Edinburgh, T. & T. Clark, 1993.

Metz, Johann Baptist, *The Emergent Church: The Future of Christianity in a Post Bourgeois World*, London, SCM, 1981.

Mitchell, Nathan, *Mission and Ministry. History and Theology in the Sacrament of Order*, Delaware, Michael Glazier, 1982.

Moltmann, Jürgen, *Jesus Christ for Today's World*, London, SCM, 1994.

—— *God for a Secular Society: The Public Relevance of Theology*, London, SCM, 1997.

Morisy, Ann, *Beyond the Good Samaritan: Community Ministry and Mission*, London, Mowbray, 1997.

Morris, Paul, *Gearing up for Mission: An All-age Mission Audit*, London, CPAS, 1995.

Northcott, Michael, *Urban Theology, A Reader*, London, Cassell, 1998.

Nietzsche, Friedrich, in O'Murchu, Diarmuid, *Reclaiming Spirituality*, Dublin, Gill and Macmillan, 1997.

Nyala, Hannah, 'Tracking the Ways of Women in Religious Leadership', in *Concillium*, London SCM, 1999/3.

O'Brien, John, *Seeds of a New Church*, Dublin, The Columba Press, 1994.

O'Halloran SDB, James, *Small Christian Communities. A Pastoral Companion*, Dublin, The Columba Press, 1996.

O'Murchu, Diarmuid, *Quantum Theology*, New York, Crossroad, 1997.

O'Siadhail, Micheal, *Poems 1975–1995*, Newcastle-upon-Tyne, Bloodaxe Books, 1999.

—— *Reclaiming Spirituality*, Dublin, Gill & Macmillan, 1997.

Pannenberg, Wolfhart, *Systematic Theology*, vol. 3, Edinburgh, T. & T. Clark, 1998. Also in Johnson, Elizabeth A., 1998.

Paton, David and Long, Charles H., *A Roland Allen Reader: The Compulsive Spirit*, Grand Rapids, Eerdmans, 1983.

Pedler, Mike, Burgoyne, John and Boydell, Tom, *The Learning Company. A Strategy for Sustainable Development*, 2nd edn, London, The McGraw-Hill Companies, 1997.

Porvoo Common Statement, *Together in Mission and Ministry*, London, Church House Publishing, 1993.

Ramsey, Michael, *The Christian Priest Today*, London, SPCK, 1972.

Report to the Methodist Conference, *The Ministry of the People of God in the World*, Peterborough, Methodist Publishing House, 1990.

Rogers, Will, in Taubman, Stan, 1994.

Rowland, Derrick, 'Team Work. Something to Talk About or Practice?' *Ministry*, the Journal of the Edward King Institute for Ministry Development, vol. 2., no. 1, Summer 1998.

Ruether, Rosemary Radford, in Grey, Mary C., 1997.

Russell, Letty, in Grey, Mary C., 1997.

St John Chrysostom, *'Good Friday Homily'*, in Grey, Mary C., 1997.

Sarton, May, in Grey, Mary C., *Beyond the Dark Night: A Way Forward for the Church?* London, Cassell, 1997.

Schillebeeckx, Edward, *Ministry: A Case for Change?* London, SCM, 1985.

—— *The Church with a Human Face*, London, SCM, 1985.

Senge, Peter M., *The Fifth Discipline: The Art and Practice of the Learning Organisation*, London, Century Business, 1993.

The Sign We Give: Report from the Working Party on Collaborative Ministry, Bishops' Conference of England and Wales, Chelmsford, Matthew James Publishing Ltd, 1995.

Skilton, Chris, *Leadership Teams: Clergy and Lay Leadership in the Local Church*, Cambridge, Grove Books Ltd, 1999.

Spriggs, David, *Christian Leadership: Growing Christian Leaders in the Local Church*, London, Bible Society, 1993.

Stephenson, Kenneth, *The Mystery of Baptism in the Anglican Tradition*, Norwich, Canterbury Press, 1998.

Stone, David, *The Baptism Service. A Guide*, London, Hodder & Stoughton, 1998.

Stranger in the Wings: A Report on Local Non-Stipendiary Ministry, Advisory Board of Ministry Policy Paper No. 8, London, Church House Publishing, 1998.

Suenens, Léon-Joseph Cardinal, *Co-responsibility in the Church*, London, Burns & Oates, 1968.

Sykes, Stephen, Gunton, Colin and Hardy, Daniel W. (eds), *On Being the Church. Essays on the Christian Community*, Edinburgh, T. & T. Clark, 1989.

Taubman, Stan, *Ending the Struggle Against Yourself*, GP Putnam's Sons, New York, 1994.

Thoreau, Henry David, in Taubman, Stan, 1994.

Tiller, John, *A Strategy for the Church's Ministry*, London, Church Information Office, 1983.

Tiller, John and Birchall, Mark, *The Gospel Community and its Leadership*, London, Marshall Pickering, 1987.

Treston, Kevin, *Creative Christian Leadership, Skills for More Effective Ministry*, Mystic LT, Twenty-Third Publications, 1995.

Vardy, Lucinda, *God in All Worlds: An Anthology of Contemporary Spiritual Writing*, London, Chatto & Windus, 1995.

Visser't Hooft, W. A., in Walton, Martin, 1994.

Walton, Martin, *Marginal Communities: The Ethical Enterprise of the Followers of Jesus*, Kampen, The Netherlands, Kok Pharos, 1994.

Ward, Hannah and Wild, Jennifer, *Guard the Chaos: Finding Meaning in Change*, London, Darton, Longman & Todd, 1995.

Warren, Robert, *Building Missionary Congregations*, London, Board of Mission Occasional Paper No. 4, 1995.

—— *Launching a Missionary Congregation*, London, CPAS, 1995.

Wesley, John, in Leech, Kenneth, 1997.

Whitehead, Mick and Hazel, *Baptism Matters*, National Society/Church House Publishing, 1998.

Woolf, Virginia, *Three Guineas*, New York, Harcourt Brace, 1938.

World Council of Churches, *Baptism, Eucharist and Ministry*, Lima Texts, Geneva, 1982.

Zabriskie, Stewart, *Total Ministry*, The Alban Institute, 1995.

Zizioulas, John, *Being as Communion: Studies in Personhood and the Church*, London, Darton, Longman & Todd, 1993.